M000301996

Conversations with Robert Evans
Lawrence Grobel

Introduction
by Dustin Hoffman
14th Annual Producers Guild Awards
March 2, 2003

In a way I probably met Robert Evans before I met him. At age 11, Mr. Evans started his illustrious acting career on the *Let's Pretend* radio show, which I listened to every Saturday morning. We were destined to work together; even then we had the same taste. But it wasn't until *Marathon Man* that I met Bob formally and now I can thank him publicly for lobbying for me; for Sir Laurence Olivier, when no insurance company would insure him because of his illness; and for the creative and courageous choice of Marthe Keller, who could not speak a word of English except for phonetically learned lines when I met her for her screen test; and for bringing John Schlesinger, the irreplaceable Conrad Hall, and William Goldman's script, as well as Bob Towne, the finest writer of his generation, to write a critical scene, to the mix. Robert Evans produced *Marathon Man* in the fullest sense of the word. I never met a producer like Bob before; I never met a producer like Bob, period. To know him and to work with him is to understand the engine that put *Chinatown*, *Rosemary's Baby*, *Love Story*, *The Godfather I & II*, and other films up there on the screen and beyond, into film history. Relentless, pathologically enthusiastic, not unlike Willy Loman. As Arthur Miller put it, "He's out there on a smile and a shoeshine. A salesman's got a dream, it comes with the territory."

One day in the middle of a tough scene on *Marathon Man*, Bob approached me in between setups and in his characteristic stage whisper said, "I gotta talk to you." Motioning me to a darkened backstage area, he held out an 8-by-10 envelope that he previously held behind his back. And the following scene is forever imprinted.

He said, "You see this, you see what I have?"

"Yes, it's a script."

"No, no, no, it's not just a script." And raising his eyebrows, "This is the finest script I've read in ten years, maybe fifteen, and you're the first to get it, okay?"

"Really?"

"I swear to God, you're the first. Not Warren. Not Jack. You're the first, okay? 'Cause I want you to have it, Star." Bob liked to call the stars he worked with "Star." And when he said it, you felt like you earned it.

I said, "Thank you. Thanks."

"You gotta read it tonight, as soon as you get home, okay, Star?"

I said, "I can't read it tonight, Bob, I got so many lines to learn for tomorrow's scene, just give me a couple of days."

"Impossible. I can't. I can't wait. You know why? Because you're the first. Not Jack, not Warren. I can't hear about it. It'll be very embarassing to me. I need you to read it tonight and you gotta get back to me tomorrow. Okay, Star?"

"I can't."

"Tonight. It's important. You don't know how important this is. It's for your career. I'll be honest with you, it's for my career. This is gonna be very big. For both of us."

He pointed his finger at me, and I said, "I know. I'm the first."

"You betcha. I'll see you on the set tomorrow, my boy." And as he leaves, with a wink and a smile, he said, "You're gonna thank me, Star."

The next day as promised, Bob was back. He patiently waited for me to finish a setup. I walked over to him.

"Did you read it?"

"Yeah, yeah, I did."

"You're the first to read it, you know that."

"I know, you told me."

"It's terrific, isn't it? I told you, it's the best script I've read in ten years. I've never had reader's reports like this. We'll have our pick of directors. What'd you think?"

"Well, it didn't get to me, Bob. I didn't respond to it."

"Why not?"

"Well, I don't think it works. I think it's a bad script."

"You know what, you're absolutely right. It's a very bad script and you're gonna make it a good script. You're gonna fix it. We're gonna both fix it. Just remember I gave it to you first. We're gonna fix it, and it's gonna be terrific, it's gonna be a home run."

That's a true story.

I don't remember the name of the script, I don't know if it got made or not. It doesn't matter. What does matter is that this was the same engine, the same enthusiasm that gave birth to all those films you just saw up there on the screen. A producer's got a dream, it comes with the territory. Bob Evans is simply a man of dreams, a man of heart, a man of passion, a man who loves films, and making films, as much if not more than anyone in this room.

In his notes on *Death of a Salesman*, Arthur Miller said that his play came from images: "The image of aging, and so many of your friends already gone, and strangers in the seats of the mighty, who do not know you, or your triumphs, or your incredible value. Above all, perhaps, the image of a need greater than hunger or sex or thirst, a need to leave a thumbprint somewhere on the world. The need for immortality, and by admitting it, the knowing that one has carefully inscribed one's name on a cake of ice on a hot July day." Bob understands this irony. He has always understood it. It's what makes him Bob.

On his notes to himself about himself in his book, Bob said, "Where is everyone? Dead? Mostly. Wealthy? Some. Destitute? Many. Retired? Uh, supposedly, I ain't seen 'em. One thing I do know, I ain't dead, I ain't wealthy, I ain't destitute, and I ain't retired."

It is with deep pleasure that I present the 2003 David O. Selznick Lifetime Achievement Award to the kid who stayed in the picture, Robert Evans.

Part 1
Wednesday, May 5, 1993

The first time I met Robert Evans at his office at Paramount Studios, in the summer of 1993, he was sitting behind a round glass table looking at ad copy for *Sliver*, which was about to open. When I entered, he didn't look up, just started talking. I leaned over the table and offered my hand, which he took, but with a puzzled look. "I want you to see this spread," he said, flipping wildly through *Us* until he found the two-page introduction to the summer movie section. He tossed the magazine in front of me. "Look at that," he crowed. "That would make a great ad. It's a hell of a lot better than the ad we've got." I glanced down at the shot of William Baldwin embracing Sharon Stone. Above, the words "Summer Heat" were written in bold red against a bright yellow background. "What do you think?"

"Looks good to me," I said.

"So, you can do it?"

"Do what?"

"Change what we've got to this."

"You'd probably have to get permission from the magazine," I said.

"Why? It's our still. Why can't you do it?"

I suddenly realized that he didn't know who I was. His secretary had come in before me, but he wasn't listening because he was expecting the head of the ad department. That's why he looked at me queerly when I went to shake his hand.

"I'm not who you think I am," I said.

Now Evans was off balance. If I wasn't the ad person, then who the hell was I? And what was I doing in his office?

"I'm here to interview you."

Evans's face began to wobble. He seemed embarrassed, but just for a moment. Then the woman from the ad department arrived and said she'd look into making the changes he wanted by the end of the day. Later she returned with the ad and he noticed how minuscule the credit type was. "Isn't that too small?" he asked. "The part with the names, my name included? I mean, contractually shouldn't it be 50 percent?"

"Not really," the woman said. "It's never more than 30 percent."

"What is it now?"

"Twenty."

"I think you're wrong. It's got to be bigger." The woman made a note and said she'd check with the lawyers. Evans turned to me and smiled.

It was a smile that said he was back, with a multi-picture deal, in his old office at Paramount, and he was glad to be there. Just four years earlier people had been saying that Hollywood had passed Evans by, that he was a relic of another generation. Sure, he was head of the studio during its heyday in the late sixties and early seventies when pictures like *Rosemary's Baby*, *Love Story*, *The Godfather* I & II, *The Odd Couple*, *True Grit*, *Paper Moon*, and *Chinatown* were made. But that was all behind him. As were his marriages to three actresses (Sharon Hugueny, Camilla Sparv, Ali McGraw) and one sportscaster and former Miss America (Phyllis George).

By 1980 he had been busted for cocaine and was on a downward decline. It was a sour decade for Evans, culminating in the suspicion that he was involved in the murder of a man named Roy Radin, who wanted to be his partner on *The Cotton Club*. It was a convoluted story: Evans, in need of financing, wound up dealing with drug dealers, arms dealers, gangsters...a lot of bad people. And when one of those bad people didn't like the way Radin was trying to isolate Evans, she supposedly had him offed. Evans had nothing to do with it, but his name was dragged into the story, which brought international attention. And after the disastrous failure of *The Cotton Club*, it was generally assumed that Robert Evans was no longer viable.

But Evans is a man who thrives on challenges and loves to be a player. So he went in search of a property that would bring him back and came up with *The Saint*. He went around the world tying up all the rights to the books, the films, the TV shows, then came back and presented it to Paramount. It was a potential industry in itself, he said. Think of Bond, of Indiana Jones. And Paramount bought it. The studio gave him back his office and made a five-picture deal with him. *The Saint*, with Val Kilmer, would eventually flop, as would *Sliver*, with Sharon Stone. Evans had worked wonders with Ira Levin's *Rosemary's Baby* in 1968, but he couldn't do it again with the same author and that year's hottest actress. Would the Comeback Kid rise again like a phoenix? Evans had no doubt about it. No doubt at all.

Do you work more at this office or at home?

I work mostly here. I have meetings at night at home and work with writers at home. My house is very conducive to working.

How much business got done at your house during the seventies?

There were more deals made in my projection room than there were at Paramount during those days. My home has made Paramount more than $1 billion. Charlie Bluhdorn and Marty Davis used to come out here and work out of my house. There were many clandestine deals because of antitrust laws, both legal and illegal, where people weren't supposed to be in the country and they were having private meetings at my house. Bluhdorn used my home as Gulf & Western West.

Who were some of the people that weren't supposed to be in the country? Can you talk about that now?

I can't, because they were private deals that were being made.

Brando told me about harboring Native American activist Dennis Banks at his home and in Tahiti when he was avoiding the FBI.

Well, for example, the deal for CIC [Cinema International Corporation] when Universal and Paramount bought out Kirk Kerkorian and all the distribution people, they bought out all of Kerkorian's theaters around the world when he owned Metro at the time and business was very bad. Lew Wasserman, Jim Aubrey, Kirk Kerkorian, Charlie

Bluhdorn, Martin Davis, myself—met at my house all weekend, back and forth. Kirk Kerkorian walked out six different times, and Charlie Bluhdorn ran down the long driveway to catch him and bring him back, and by the end of the weekend the deal was closed.

Warren Beatty, myself, Jack Nicholson, Sue Mengers, Bob Towne, we always used to sit around casting pictures. I'd like to show you a tape about myself that might help you, if I may put it on.

No, no, let's keep talking. I can see it later.

It tells you very much about the house. I'll give you the tape, okay?

Fine. But why don't you tell me about the people who come to your house.

In my screening room Jack Nicholson comes four or five times a week looking at pictures; a lot of directors come to look at their films. *The Godfather* was edited there, *The Two Jakes.* I can go on and on. A couple of years ago I needed new chairs. The old chairs were there for twenty-two years, cotton was coming out of them, it looked like the Salvation Army. I designed a chair and got six of them made and put them in. Nicholson comes over and asks, "Where are the old chairs?" I said I was looking to give them away to the Motion Picture Relief Home so I could get a write-off on them. He said he wanted them. So he sent down a truck and had them picked up. Two weeks later he comes back and says to me, "You gave me the greatest gift I ever got. Those chairs. They're the most valuable chairs in all of Hollywood history. Do you know what happened in those chairs over the last twenty-five years? Mike Nichols wants one, Meryl, Warren, Bernardo...everyone wants a chair." I didn't know what I owned. He said, "I may give one to Meryl and to Bernardo. I'm not giving one to Warren." Suddenly I didn't like my new chairs anymore. And Jack won't give me back the old ones [*laughs*].

What has he given you in exchange?

Loyalty. That he's given to me like no one else.

According to the book The Club Rules, *you are the producer with the most mystique, though no one knows why. Do you?*

I'm a loner, that's why. When I was head of Paramount I had a contract that said I didn't have to go out to parties, I didn't have to go to functions. I could always assign someone, from the Academy Awards to the MPAA [Motion Picture Association of America] meetings. I just wanted to be involved with film. It's strange. I was invited to a meeting that Lew Wasserman was having at his house, and I didn't show up. He called me, very angry, and he said, "Why aren't you here?" And I said, "I'm editing *The Godfather*, that's why." He said, "That's what editors do. You get over here to the meeting, that's your responsibility." I didn't care. I never showed. He must have been right and I was wrong, because he's counting his millions by the hundreds and I'm looking at the millions I owe in the tens. But I only cared about the film. I was a lousy executive. I designated the political and corporate matters to others, but I did care about the minutiae of film. And product-wise, I turned the product around in the company.

Totally different. We were four people who ran the company in those days: Marty Davis, Stanley Jaffe, Peter Bart, and myself. I ran it out in California with Peter as my associate, and Marty and Stanley were in New York. We had a hundred actors around. Now there are a hundred executives and four actors around. That's the best way I can say it. It's a whole different business. It's a committee business, it's a distribution business—you make a picture to make a date, you don't make a picture to make it good. Do I like it? I *hate* it. On my knees glad I'm here? I'm on my knees I'm glad I'm here. Because this is the only game in town.

And all the studios are the same. There is no such word as an "independent" producer. Everyone is a dependent producer. That's the biggest misnomer in the entire film library, that word. The only time that you're an independent producer is when you use your own money. Sam Goldwyn was an independent producer. He spent $6 million of his own money and made *Guys and Dolls*. He owned it, he could do what he wanted, he could tell people to fuck off. When you're being paid—overpaid, as everybody in this business is, including myself—you take the orders. You're not independent.

When I ran the company, it was so different because it went through me, I said yes or no, and there was no one else. We made twenty to twenty-five pictures a year with only two people here. Now there are fifty people here, and they can't get ten pictures made. Why? I don't know. It's become a commodity rather than an art form. And everything is researched, which is nauseating. If a picture goes up three points in a confined period, that's a better picture. It has nothing to do with the quality of the film.

I don't believe in the way they test pictures today at all. It's totally wrong. I believe that a picture has to go out where people spend their two bucks. I'll give you an example. When we took *Marathon Man* out to be previewed, John Schlesinger said, "I will not preview a film." I insisted that he did. We took it to San Francisco. He said, "Well, I shan't change a frame." In the middle of the picture someone stood up and said, "You should be ashamed of yourself, this is a disgrace!" By the end of the picture they almost threw our car over when we walked out of the theater. We didn't make one change—we made a hundred and ten changes!

Here, if you preview a picture, it's an invited audience. You don't get your highs, you don't get your lows. And you don't know how good or bad the picture is. It's no different than if you come to my house for dinner and my food is lousy but you can't say, "Send it back, I can't eat it." But if you and I went over to Chasen's and the food was lousy, you can say, "Send it back, it's no good." When you pay for it, you can criticize. When you're invited, you can't.

Are films at all better now than they were twenty-five years ago?

They're not nearly as good. I looked at the pictures when *Chinatown* was up for an Academy Award. There was *Chinatown*, *Lenny*, *Godfather II*, *The Conversation*, and *A Woman Under the Influence*. Each one of those pictures was really extraordinary. And you look at the pictures up for an Academy Award today, it's tough to pick five. Today, distribution runs the film business. Maybe because it's so expensive, and the numbers are so big today, and the swings are so big. It seems that it's more and more difficult to put pictures together.

I've been a success in whatever I've done. I've never looked at things any other way. The toughest time has been the last five years. It's easy at 20 to be hopeful, but when you're approaching 60 and you're on your ass, you have two places to go: one, the Motion Picture Relief Home, or two, down to live in Palm Springs. When you're successful at my age, it's difficult to stay there, because I'm considered too old. To make a comeback at my age... it's like getting out of the grave.

To get back is much more difficult than to get there. This office I'm in now...I had a party a year ago Christmas moving back onto the lot. Three years before that I couldn't get into the commissary. I invited everybody from the guards to the Xerox operators to the secretaries to the chairman of the board to Warren Beatty, Jack Nicholson, Raquel Welch—they were all here, more than three hundred people. I had a Christmas tree and a present for everybody: a box with a candle, a lighter, and a fake hundred-dollar bill around it, and a saying: "May you open this and may it give you health, love, and a little extra green for the New Year." And Jack and I stood outside in front of the awning, and he looked at me and he said, "You know, kid, you're ten thousand to one." That was the miracle in my life. Not getting to where I was. But getting back.

It's tough to get up the ladder, but the higher you climb the farther down you fall. And everyone always wants to see you fall.

I was thrown out of this office in 1987. I had been here for fifteen years. I was thrown out because I turned down a million dollars to do an Eddie Murphy film. I'm not that kind of producer. I'm not going to be there to say, "Yes, ma'am." Instead, I made something that I'm proudest of in my entire career: *The Planet is Alive*, America's gift to His Holiness—for the Pope. And everyone thought I was crazy. I put $1.4 million of my own money in it.

Interesting that the man who produced The Godfather *films says that, since those two films are among the greatest movies ever made.*

Filmic-wise, *The Godfather* and *Love Story* are the two for me. The reason I say *Love Story* is, it's a total aphrodisiac. There were more pregnancies from that picture than any other ever made in the history of film. And I was witness to it. Guys would bring a different girl every night, and for that night they were in love. I'm the only producer still alive who has two pictures—*The Godfather* and *Chinatown*—selected by the Library of Congress to be among the seventy-five films of the twentieth century to be put in a vault for perpetuity.

Why do abnormal people make good actors?

Very good reason: People are not interested in watching normalcy on the screen; it's boring. They see it in life. You have to have a certain craziness, be a little different, otherwise you're not interesting to watch. Interesting to be with possibly. Actors to me aren't interesting people. Most of them are introverted, very dull, scared. But they hold back their real lives and can only act it out in their fantasies. Why, when Jack Nicholson walks on and smiles, does the screen light up? Why can Al Pacino, who's 5 foot 6, stand next to a guy 6 foot 3 on the screen and you don't even see the other guy? Something about him. Nothing to do with size, it's presence. Something offbeat, quirky.

Voices are very important. A voicebox is the most important part of any actor or actress. Humphrey Bogart's lisp, Clark Gable had his voice, Jack Nicholson, Faye Dunaway, Katharine Hepburn...you remember their voices. Not the measurements of their height, their breasts, their beautiful looks—that doesn't mean anything. Presence is a strange thing, and it has nothing to do with cosmetic beauty. Nothing.

Marlon Brando never could remember his lines, never studied them well. He's brilliant, though, because he's a presence. He's crazy. Jack Nicholson will be remembered—where actors like Kevin Costner, who's a wonderful actor, won't be after twenty years—because Jack has that crazy look about him. That's why Bogie is and Robert Taylor isn't. Jimmy Cagney is remembered, where Tyrone Power won't be.

Do producers also expect to be remembered the way actors do?

"Producer" is a lousy word today. A producer gets so little respect. He's like Willy Loman. I really feel that way. A producer is on a project longer than anybody else. He usually buys the property, hires the writer, the director, is involved in the production, the post-production, the marketing, and he gets very little credit.

Isn't that because there's such confusion about exactly what a producer does, since there're so many different titles: executive producer, associate producer, assistant producer, line producer, etc.?

No one knows what a producer is. Because a producer

means many things: He can be a dealmaker, an agent, the husband or wife of someone. But a real producer, like David Selznick, Darryl Zanuck, Sam Spiegel, a director needs him.

Why single out the director?

Because a movie has to be a vision that the two creators see. It has to be that the director and the producer see the same picture, and they should help each other. Very few directors have respect for producers, because they're usually dealmakers. The best thing a director can have is a producer who protects him. And the best thing they can have for each other is friction throughout the piece. Because through that friction and grit comes some-thing great. But when the front office is stepping in and everyone has an opinion and they write thirty pages of notes for every junior executive, it's counterproductive.

Since no one knows what a producer does, on a sliding scale of low to high, which side are you on?

I'm on the *very* good side of it, and I'm proud to say it. I'm *fucking* good at what I do. I work too hard and give too much of myself. I ruined my personal life, to the detri-ment of my own health. I ended up in the hospital twice. They thought I had a heart attack two months ago. They gave me an angiogram. Fortunately there wasn't anything wrong. My blood pressure was up to 215. I couldn't catch my breath.

Critic Richard Schickel said that all of your movies suffer from over-production: "Obsession with details can ruin a picture."

I don't think anything I've done has been overly produced. I like things not to be overly produced. I think background makes foreground. The difference between The Great Gatsby and Chinatown was ten minutes into Gatsby you knew you were in the period, and Chinatown seeps through. If you call looking for perfection overproduction, then I overproduce. I'm very reverent toward what I have and want to make things better. If that's overproduction, then I overproduce.

What's the biggest chance you've ever taken?

I took a chance becoming the head of the studio when I had never produced a film. I was there to produce The Detective, and circumstance gave me the chance to become the head of Paramount. I was the laughingstock of the whole city.

The Detective was for Fox, wasn't it?

Which they would have bought from me for half a million. They wanted the property, but I said I wouldn't give it to them unless I got not only offices on the lot but I wanted my picture put in the trade papers attaching me to the project. When you have them, you've got to take the chance to blow a deal, otherwise you'll never make it. I made three other deals while I was there—all controversial projects. One was the life of Maurice Chevalier; another was the F. Lee Bailey story about the Sam Sheppard murders. I had so much going as a kid there without having made one picture that Peter Bart, who was writing for the Sunday New York Times, wrote an article in the Arts & Leisure section about this young producer who in four months had more projects going than anyone in Hollywood. Charlie Bluhdorn had just bought Paramount at the time, and he read this article. And to make a very long story short, I became the head of Paramount Studios before I started my first movie.

Before this, didn't you spend some months in London as head of production for Paramount?

They sent me to London first because the action was there. It was the mid-sixties, and that's when *Georgy Girl*, *Alfie*, all the hot talent was there. Then they moved me here, and I was a laughingstock. I was called Bluhdorn's Folly. They thought I'd last three days. *Variety* said I'd be fired at the end of the month. I called Bluhdorn once after I had read that I was being let go, and I got him out of a meeting in Spain to ask if I was being fired. "Listen carefully, Evans," he said. "As long as I own Paramount, you're head of the studio, unless you call me like this again." And he hung the phone up.

Why was Charlie Bluhdorn so confident in you?

Sense of discovery. I was his pick. And he backed me all the way.

Did you have your own doubts?

Never. I always believed in myself. But I believe I could walk on a court and beat Jimmy Connors in tennis and I won't get a point. You've got to believe in yourself.

Was Bluhdorn a surrogate father figure?

No, not in any way. He was my Knute Rockne. He believed in you and backed you. He was an emotional animal and an entrepreneurial person. He was a unique, brilliant human being.

How much influence did he have on your decision making?

I fought him on everything. When I first came to the company, I got a call from Charlie Feldman, a close friend of mine who was an agent and also produced *Casino Royale* and *What's New, Pussycat?* He told me to come see him on a Sunday morning, and when I got there he said, "I'm gonna make you a winner, kid. *Funny Girl* has just fallen out of Columbia. The bank isn't giving them the money to make it, and I'm ready to give it to you, it'll make you a star." Ray Stark comes in and says he can't do it at Paramount because he doesn't get along with Bluhdorn, and Feldman says, "Ya gotta do it for Bobby. I want him to have *Funny Girl*." So Stark says he'll give me forty-eight hours. I rush home and call Bluhdorn. There were only two hours a week when no one could disturb him, and that was on Sunday afternoon when he would take a hot bath. I took him out of his hot bath and said, "Charlie, listen carefully. I've got *Funny Girl*." He said, "You're crazy, you can't have it." I said I had it, there's a freak thing happening that Columbia doesn't have the money to make it and we can get it but I have to answer in forty-eight hours. Charlie says, "That's my favorite show, I've seen it six times. Stay where you are." He got on the phone and called distribution all over the world, then called me back later that night and said, "We can't go forward with it. No one wants to make it with Barbra Streisand. If Shirley MacLaine would do it that's something else. But no one wants to see that

Jewish girl in a picture." I said, "Charlie, don't listen to them. It's your favorite show, it's my favorite show, we've got to do it." He said, "Bob, if you were here a little longer I'd go along with you, but you just came here, it's a very big project, and not one person I talked with wants to do it." "Go on your own instincts, Charlie," I said. "We're never going to have anything better than *Funny Girl*." But he wouldn't do it. Instead we made *Darling Lili*, which almost put us out of business. But from that time on he believed in my instincts.

Does Streisand know this story?

Sure she does. And we made *On a Clear Day You Can See Forever* with her, which was a disaster.

Is it true you offered to let families in for free to Darling Lili *and still no one came?*

That's right. In those days the film business was at its all-time low. Pornography had just come in. The Pussycat Theaters were opening all over the country. In New York *Darling Lili* was playing at Radio City with no one in the theater, and a Pussycat Theater had people around the block trying to get in. It was a real distressing time. We just about sold the studio. By one vote did it miss being sold to become a cemetery. Instead, we ended up buying Desilu for next to nothing. As well as Simon & Schuster, which I bought for the company for $10 million; they later sold 75 percent of it for $4 billion. My bonus for it was a trip to Miami...coach.

Did Blake Edwards challenge you to a fight during the production of Darling Lili?

Yeah. And I'd love to have fought him, too. When people challenge you to a fight, they don't throw the punch.

Have you been in many physical fights?

A lot. I fought in the Golden Gloves. I'm a rough guy. I'm afraid of nothing. I'm not afraid of being killed.

Doesn't everyone have some fear?

I don't want to have a slow death. That's my fear. I've had a gun put in my mouth, a gun put at my temple. I won't talk about it, but I can tell you I've had a gun put on me five different times to talk, and not once have I ever talked. The last couple of times it hasn't bothered me because I was too well known for them to have blown me away. Stanley Jaffe said to me, "Why is it that whenever you get involved with anything there's drama?" It happened again with *Sliver*. Look what's happened here: Bill MacDonald, my associate, ends up with Sharon Stone; Joe Eszterhas is ending up with Bill's wife. Wherever I am there's an incident. I'm very incident-prone. Some people are accident-prone, some are health-prone, I'm incident-prone.

I've always had a theory that has kept me poor but has given me a wealth of some kind. I like making deals with people where they've got the better of the deal. Because they'll always come back. Barry Diller said to me once, about fifteen years ago, "You know, Evans, you're never going to be rich. You're very bright, you're tenacious, you're talented as any producer I know, but you'll never have any money because you totally lack greed." And I do. I don't care about being the richest guy on the block, it matters the least to me.

Which of the deadly sins affects you the most?

I like living well. I like seeing things blossom. That's my turn-on.

When you first came to Paramount, you had to fire a lot of people, you didn't fill old jobs, and rather than look to the more established talent you went with new, younger talent. How courageous was that?

We moved off the studio lot. The single most popular man in Hollywood was at Paramount: Howard Koch. That's why he produced many of the Academy Award shows, because he could get anyone on them. Everyone loved Howard. To put me in and take Howard out, from the guards to the secretaries everyone hated me. They laughed at me. Hal Wallis, Otto Preminger, they all had to report to me. I had to take the prima donnas on like you can't imagine. There were eight studios, and we were ninth when I came here. The biggest stars we had were [the comedy team] Allen & Rossi. I was greeted with skepticism and disdain. But there's an old saying: When your back's against the wall, the impossible becomes possible. And I wanted to prove that Charlie Bluhdorn was right in backing me.

I wanted to make a picture about an 18-year-old boy who falls in love with an 80-year-old woman, *Harold and Maude.* How do you explain that to anybody? They wanted to throw me out of here. They thought I was crazy.

Didn't you fly to Lucerne to meet with Vladimir Nabokov when his novel Ada was still in manuscript?

I always wanted to buy a literary piece of material, and he was my favorite author. *Laughter in the Dark* and *Lolita* were wonderful books. Irving Lazar was his agent, and he said, "Kid, I'm going to give you a break. Nabokov has just finished his new novel, and he lives in Lucerne. Get on the plane and fly over, and you'll be the first to look at it." I fly there. It's eleven in the morning, and there's this long dining room with two old people sitting there, Nabokov and his wife. He said, "You can't be the head of the studio." Because when you're 80 years old...I look to him about 16. I had to prove to him that I was the head. We ate breakfast, and he gave me this huge manuscript to read. I go up to the room, and we're supposed to meet the next morning for breakfast. And I read and read, and I don't understand anything. I take a Dexamil to stay awake because I think I'm hallucinating. If I had to describe what the book was about, I couldn't talk about it. Now everybody at Paramount—Marty Davis, Bluhdorn—they're desperately waiting. The next morning I come down and I say, "It's extraordinary, I never read anything quite like it." I didn't know what to say.

I fly back to New York and meet with Charlie and Marty, and I say, "Fellas, I don't know how to tell you this: I don't know what I read." Marty says to Charlie, "I told you the kid doesn't know what he's doing." I said, "You know something, Marty, I produced one play when I was an actor, something I read but didn't understand, but I raised the money anyway, and we closed in Philadelphia after one night. I learned when I read something and I don't understand it, let someone else have the success. I can't lie to you, I don't know what it's all about."

Two weeks later Columbia buys it, and they say, "You should have bought it, why didn't you buy it?" Well, Columbia didn't understand it either. They never made it.

And when you do understand material, is it easier to buy?

No one wanted to make *Love Story.* Everyone said, "What kind of piece of shit, pulp junk, is this?" I cried when I read it. I wrote the book with Erich Segal. No one wanted to print the book. They printed 6,000 copies. They were going to give it away as a throwaway. I offered them $25,000 for advertising if they printed 25,000 books. So they did it, and it became the No. 1 bestseller of the decade.

It was originally a screenplay before it was a book. How did you know to make it a book first?

That's instinct. You can't buy it, you don't learn it, you don't inherit it. You either have it or you don't. *The Godfather* was a thirty-page treatment called "The Mafia." We owned these properties. In 1970 the studio was going to close and move to New York. I turned in my resignation. I had Mike Nichols shooting *Catch-22* at the time, and I had him do something for me, and I went to New York with this tape. I said to the board, "I'm sorry business is going so terrible. I don't want anything for my severance, I'll sign off now, but I just want you to watch something that I just put together, what I believe Paramount is all about." And I put on this tape for the eighteen directors on the board of Gulf & Western, and Marty Davis backed me on this, and it turned things around. [*Shows me the tape: Evans talks into the camera, introducing some of the upcoming* films Paramount was shooting at the time: A New Leaf, The Confession, Deadhead Miles (with Alan Arkin), Plaza Suite, Love Story.]

Within six years you turned Paramount around...

What brought us over the top was Love Story, The Godfather, True Grit—there were six or seven big hits, and suddenly from being no one we were the biggest studio in the industry.

Yet you rate yourself as a lousy executive.

I'm a terrible executive. I'm terrible at financial things; that's why I have no money.

Is it because you could concentrate on only one or two pictures a year?

I focused on four or five pictures that I took over each year and believed in from their conception. That's my problem. I can't make many pictures. I spend so much time, I get impassioned. To do a Harold and Maude you had to have belief in it, it was such a crazy idea. Romeo and Juliet was another one.

Is there anybody like you that you know?

No.

How about Streisand?

Barbra is absolutely that way. She's impassioned. But

she's a very wealthy woman because she's a talented actress and a singer. I'm not. That's why I have no money. I spend so much time on just one project. And you can spend just as much time on a failure as on a success. That's what Lew Wasserman criticized me for. But I couldn't help it.

Wasn't it on that Streisand picture, On a Clear Day You Can See Forever, *when you first met Nicholson?*

Let me give you a great Jack Nicholson story. I'm making *On a Clear Day.* Barbra Streisand has signed on for the picture with Yves Montand. This is a wonderful story. There's the part of Tad, Streisand's half-brother. I looked at fifty actors for the part, and I saw this one guy and asked who it was. The head of casting and talent wanted me to look at someone else, but I kept going back to this guy with a smile. "Find out who the guy with the smile is," I said. Comes back the next day and says, "Some nut named Nicholson, works for Roger Corman." I said I wanted to meet him. But he was in Cannes, he had just finished making two pictures, each one cost $6,000. One was *House of Horrors*, and the other he starred in, produced, and directed. But I'm told he's crazy and I should forget about it. I had to fly to New York, and I got a call from an agent who said Jack Nicholson was in town. "Who's that?" I asked. "The guy with the smile," he said. "Oh, that guy. Have him come over to the Sherry, I'll meet him." We hadn't cast the part yet. He walked in with the agent, and this is why I love working at home and not an office. I learned this from Darryl Zanuck. We're sitting and talking for a while, and I said to him, "You know, kid, I loved your smile. I'm going to star you with Barbra Streisand

and Yves Montand in *On a Clear Day*, and I'm going to pay you $10,000 for six weeks' work."

He smiled and said, "That's great, but I just finished a picture called *Easy Rider*..." I said, "I don't want to hear about that shit, another motorcycle picture. This is Barbra Streisand. You'll be singing a song with her." His agent said, "Shut up, Jack, let Mr. Evans talk." I said, "No, let him talk." So Nicholson said, "Can I talk to you alone, Mr. Evans?" We walked to the window of the Sherry, it was snowing out, and he looked at me and said, "You know, pal, I just got divorced, I got a kid, I've got no money to pay alimony or child support. Can you make it fifteen?" I said, "How about twelve-five?" "Do you mean it?" he asked. And we hugged and kissed. And that's how we met. And we have remained friends ever since.

That could never have happened in an office. Because when you're sitting behind a desk, it's intimidating. Here we are sitting with our feet up on the couch and we could talk. Darryl Zanuck never wanted to meet with writers or artists in an office, because it was adversarial.

Let's go back to your very first deal once you were in that position of power at Paramount: Was it The President's Analyst with James Coburn?

Yes. And the FBI came to me before the picture started. They came at J. Edgar Hoover's request. They said that the FBI was talked about in the script very unattractively and I had to change it. I said I wouldn't. They said, "We advise you very strongly. Mr. Hoover's asking you to change it." I said, "Tell Hoover to go fuck himself!" I got a call from Charlie Bluhdorn. "Bob, please don't cause trouble." So I acquiesced and changed the name to the FBE. And my phone has been tapped ever since.

When you made this first decision, was it harder than any of the others?

No, I always want to do the offbeat. I wanted to do the unexpected. I wanted to be a trendsetter rather than a trend follower. When I had *Rosemary's Baby*, people thought I was crazy. When I made *Goodbye Columbus*, I used an unknown actress, an unknown director, an unknown producer, Stanley Jaffe...and I loved it. I love people stories.

Did you know Ali McGraw then?

No. But I fell in love with her watching the dailies. She didn't want to have anything to do with me. She had been living with a guy for three years, had no interest in me at all, disliked everything I stood for. She was a real bohemian. She was the one who gave me *Love Story* and no one wanted to make it. I flipped her for it. I got her to fly out for one night to look at Arthur Hiller's *The Out-of-Towners*. She came here, never saw the movie, never left my house. Until she dumped me three years later.

Let's look at what excited you about the other films you gave the okay to. I'll name the picture, you say what comes into your head. The Odd Couple.

The Odd Couple was the first confrontation I had with Paramount. Paramount then was looked upon as a B studio. For *The Odd Couple* they wanted to put in Jack Klugman and Tony Randall for the movie. And I wanted Jack Lemmon

24

and Walter Matthau, who wanted a million dollars. Billy Wilder was locked in. William Morris controlled the three of them. And Bluhdorn and Marty Davis flew out from New York. We met at my house for three days, it was like a brothel, with guys coming in and out. I insisted on having Lemmon and Matthau, and they didn't want to spend the money. Well, we couldn't afford Lemmon, Matthau, and Wilder. So Jack and Walter fucked Billy Wilder over, and he was left out of the package. But that was the start of the turnaround. I got Lemmon and Matthau.

Paint Your Wagon.

That was Charlie Bluhdorn's desire.

The Little Prince, which you thought would be The Wizard of Oz *of the seventies.*

It should have been. I brought Lerner and Lowe back together again; they had broken up. They wrote the most beautiful score for it. Stanley Donen directed it. Frank Sinatra was ready to come out of retirement to play the part, but Stanley wouldn't work with him. Then Richard Burton wanted to play it. He sang beautifully, but Stanley didn't want to work with Burton. It should have been wonderful. I loved it, but it didn't turn out well. It was a big disappointment. No one went to see it. It played to empty theaters. But the picture was good. Bob Fosse had a wonderful piece in it. Gene Wilder. It was a dream that didn't come true.

Blue, which was supposed to star Robert Redford.

Blue was one of the biggest disasters of all time. Redford walked off four days before it was to start and disappeared. Two years later he was going to do *Rosemary's Baby*, and Roman Polanski had a meeting with him, and someone served Redford with a subpoena because of *Blue*. We lost Redford because of that.

The Molly Maguires, *with Sean Connery and Richard Harris.*

Disaster! An expensive picture. The only place that it did business was in Pittsburgh. It was about the coal business, and it was a big mistake.

Paper Moon.

Wonderful, I loved it. No one would make it. The only way Peter [Bogdanovich] would make it was if he could use Tatum O'Neal, who never did a part. He line-fed her. And Ryan [O' Neal] was terrific in it. I'm so proud of that one.

Lady Sings the Blues.

I love to make integrated pictures. I had a very bad back and had a stretcher in my projection room. Berry Gordy and I reedited the entire film. It was a success, but it didn't do as much business as it should have. Diana Ross was nominated for an Academy Award. I'm very proud of that film. And it had all to do with me because no one wanted to make it. They didn't want to make a black picture.

I had a project that I was going to make called *I Love You*. It started and ended on New Year's Eve. I was going to direct it as well. It was about a black girl, a Kelly girl, who meets this guy in Atlanta who's the head of Coca-

Cola, a young guy from the wrong side of the tracks, who arrives back from Peking where he closed the deal in China to sell Coca-Cola. It's New Year's Eve, and he belongs to the Riding Club, this top country club that is so restrictive they don't even allow a black senator there. It tells of their romance, and the next New Year's Eve he walks in there, knowing that his career is over, and he says to her, "I don't care, I love you." Those three words. I signed Beverly Johnson to do the part because I wanted to get a black girl who was more beautiful than any white girl in any room, and she was that. And I couldn't get a white actor to play opposite her to get the picture made. That was when Jimmy Carter got in, in 1976. The reason I wanted to make it was that I resented the fact that Jimmy Carter got in because of the black vote and he was the most conservative Southerner.

True Grit.

I loved. No one wanted to see John Wayne with a patch over his eye. Hal Wallis and I said, "We've got to make this picture." Duke and I were very friendly. He won the Academy Award for it.

Catch-22.

I thought that was brilliant. But it was too sophisticated.

In Chinatown Faye Dunaway credits you with changing the music for her love scene with Nicholson, and it making all the difference.

It did.

They disagreed on the ending: Robert Towne thought John Huston's character should be killed, you and Roman Polanski wanted Dunaway killed. Would the picture have been as memorable if Towne got his way?

Never. Never!

Is Towne still angry about it?

Of course.

And what about John Huston? Did you know him before?

I spent some time with John. I liked him. I knew him through Toots as well—Anjelica [Huston]. John was wonderful in that film.

Did he ever have any ideas that he offered?

He stayed out of it.

Whose idea was it to do The Godfather as a period family chronicle rather than another gangster movie?

Francis [Ford Coppola] wanted to show capitalism in America. When I hired Francis, Dick Zanuck and John Calley both called me and told me I was going to be fired from my job. Dick said, "Bob, they're going to throw you off the picture, the guy's nuts." Calley called me and said American Zoetrope owed them $600,000. "We get all his money. You're my friend, you made Catch-22 with me. Don't use him, Bob, you don't know the problems you're going to get into." He had made only three pictures at that time: *You're a*

Big Boy Now, which did no business; *Finian's Rainbow*, which was a disaster; and *Rain People*, which was a slow art film.

So why did you choose Coppola?

For one reason. He was the only Italian director in Hollywood. And I wanted it told from the viewpoint of a second-generation Italian. I made a very careful study. Even after I developed it from a thirty-page treatment into the biggest best seller of the decade, Paramount did not want to make it. Because there had not been one Mafia film ever made that had made a profit, including *The Brotherhood*, which Paramount had made two years before. They had been written, directed, and acted by Jews. And there's a thin line between a Jew and a Sicilian, so that's why I went with Coppola. Because I wanted to smell the spaghetti.

Did you want to replace Coppola with Elia Kazan?

No. At first, because everyone was complaining about Coppola not knowing what he was doing, I called Gadge [Kazan]. He said, "Stick with Francis."

Coppola claims he was fired three times from the picture.

Four. I fired him at the beginning of the film. Two weeks into shooting I got a call from the editors, who said they couldn't edit it. There's a scene where Pacino blows away Sollozzo and Sterling Hayden in the restaurant, which they said they couldn't edit. So I had the film sent to me, and I edited it over the weekend, and it was brilliant. I got on the red-eye, fired the editors, and told Francis he was brilliant. But he was so shaken at the time, no one believed in him. He almost had a nervous breakdown. Charlie Bluhdorn came in and kept him up. When the picture was finished, however, and he edited the film and I saw it, I said it was not releasable. He had taken out all the texture. The picture was supposed to open that Christmas, and I went to the Paramount hierarchy and said, we cannot open it then. I almost lost my job over it. They pushed it back, and we added fifty minutes to the picture.

What was your initial reaction to Pacino as Michael Corleone?

You know how Pacino got the part? I didn't want Pacino. Francis did. He didn't want Jimmy Caan, and I did. So we settled. But you know who talked me into using Pacino? Brando. Pacino didn't test well, and Brando called me. We didn't speak much, but he called me about this. He said, "Listen to me, Bob. He's a brooder. And if he's my son, that's what you need, because I'm a brooder." It was Brando's insight that made me understand why Al would work.

Was Warren Beatty your first choice for Michael Corleone?

No, I wanted Alain Delon. He was the type, but he couldn't speak English well. Maybe I did want Warren. I may have thought of Jack Nicholson too for it. Jack tells me I did, but I don't remember it. Dustin [Hoffman] desperately wanted to do it.

Did you eventually warm up to Pacino?

Al did an interview for *The Godfather*. It was the opening night, and a reporter from *Time* was to talk to him. Al was living in a cellar at the time, so he asked to use my suite at the Carlyle. He came up with a little navy pea cap, he looked like a second-story guy, and he said to me, "Can you loan me a fiver? I've got no money for a cab tonight for the opening." And I'm thinking, "This is the lead of *The Godfather?*" So I gave him two hundred-dollar bills. He puts them in his pocket and goes and does the interview.

Ever get the money back?

Of course not. You ever get anything back from an actor? Uh-uh [laughs]. Marthe Keller told me about Al, that she went with him for six years and she couldn't afford him anymore.

What ever happened to Marthe Keller? She was in Black Sunday, which you produced, but then she disappeared.

I can answer that easily: Name one European actress who's ever made it in America. You can't. The last one was Ingrid Bergman. Sophia Loren never made it in America. The only actor is Arnold Schwarzenegger. There's a reason for it. Between New York and Los Angeles there's a huge valley called the United States of America. In that valley they want to hear American spoken. Alain Delon came over here, he was the biggest European actor alive, couldn't sell him in America, he was French. Doesn't matter who it is, Anna Brazzi, Romy Schneider, Brigitte Bardot, Catherine Deneuve, you can go on and on, they never made it in America.

Speaking of foreign actors: Did you consider Carlo Ponti or Laurence Olivier for Don Corleone?

No. Marlon was a fraud in this thing. He hadn't even read the book. He needed the part. Francis did a silent test of him. Dino De Laurentiis, when he was told that Marlon was going to play the part, said he wouldn't be able to open the picture in Italy, he'd be laughed off the screen. Marlon had made twenty-two pictures before that, eleven of them were unreleasable. He was as dead as dead could be. Marlon did the part for $50,000. Everyone else got $35,000. And he had one point of the gross after the first $10 million, two points for the second, three, four, and five points up to $60 million. No picture ever did that. Norman Gary, his attorney, called me and said Marlon was desperately in need of $100,000. I told Charlie Bluhdorn, and Charlie said to give it to him but get the points back. We got the points back in twenty-four hours. That $100,000 cost him $11 million.

Did he ever try to renegotiate?

When it happened, he went crazy. And I don't blame him. He fired Norman Gary, he fired his agent. He called me and said, "I'll play the part in *Gatsby*, but I want my deal back." I said one picture has nothing to do with the other. He said, "It's the same company."

Can you compare Brando and Pacino as Godfathers?

What's so interesting seeing Brando in *The Godfather* and Al in *Godfather III* is that Marlon was two years younger than Al when he played the part, and yet he had a stature about him that was remarkable. Brando was ageless. Al was 47 when he played it, Marlon was 44.

A trip to the Virgin Islands.

And did you buy Francis a Mercedes?

Yes. I had predicted that the picture would do $50 million. He said if it did would I buy him a Mercedes. The day it did $50 million he went and bought the most expensive Mercedes he could, twelve cylinders, and charged it to me. He made it up to me ten years later. He gave me a second asshole like no one has ever given it to me in my life.

You're jumping ahead, we'll get to The Cotton Club, *but let's stay with the two* Godfather *movies.*

Let me make it real clear what happened with those. I did *The Godfather* with Francis, and we had horrendous fights. He only became the *macha* of the industry from that film; he became a genius. If his cut was shown, it would have been on television. When we made *Godfather II*, he wanted total autonomy, and he had it. I had nothing to do with it until we went to preview the picture in San Francisco two months before it was to open. When he walked into the theater, they stood up and applauded him as if he was a king. By the time the picture was over half the theater was empty. What he had done: He left out the entire Havana sequence, the Meyer Lansky-Hyman Roth scene, and had more of Sicily with subtitles. It was a *bore*. And we went back and made more than a hundred changes. We put back Havana, which was the best part of the movie. He doesn't know how to structure a movie.

And after he received his second Oscar, he didn't acknowledge you again. Was that hurtful?

On purpose. We stood at the Dorothy Chandler Pavilion in the back. Chinatown was a 6-5 favorite against the field. And he said, "You're going to win, Evans." And I said, "No, you're going to Francis. This is your year." He said, "Isn't it funny. If I win, it's because of you." I said, "I know it." He wins. I'm sitting there. He thanks everybody except me. Then to put the knife in farther, he said to me afterwards, "God, I forgot to thank you again." That's how Machiavellian he is.

If you had to do it over again, would you accept releasing the first Godfather as a lesser picture if you could still be married to Ali McGraw?

Of course I would have. My priorities were fucked up. When my son was born, I was out here editing, fighting with Francis, instead of being in New York with her.

You were a very hot couple—what went wrong with the marriage?

I fucked up the marriage. She told me before we got married, "I'm a hot lady, Evans, don't leave me for more than two weeks at a time." I left her for four months without visiting her once. Plus she was with one of the most attractive men in the world to boot [Steve McQueen]. Because I was too busy cutting the fucking Godfather. All right?

Is it true that you got Life to agree to put you and Ali and your son Joshua on the cover—and presented it to Ali as a reason for you to stay together? And she blew up?

No. *Life* wanted us to be on the cover, and Ali refused. I said fine.

Your son is in his late twenties now. What does he do?

He's an actor, director, writer. He's starting his first picture, raised $100,00 to make a movie. He comes to me all the time, not for money but for advice. He's my best friend. I didn't make him go to college, which his mother wanted. I said, go out and make it. He played Tom Cruise's kid brother in *Born on the Fourth of July*, the kid manager of the Doors in *The Doors*. Oliver Stone's crazy about him. He costarred with Denzel Washington and John Lithgow in *Ricochet*. He can't take the shit of being an actor, though. So he's writing and directing now and using my house as a location.

Brando could never take the shit of being an actor and look what he did. He followed The Godfather *with* Last Tango in Paris. *Did you have a shot at that?*

I was going to do *Last Tango in Paris*. *The Godfather* hadn't come out yet. Everybody turned it down, Alain Delon, Jean-Paul Belmondo, but Brando took it. And I knew how great it was. Yet Paramount wouldn't make the deal because it was an X-rated picture.

Have you ever been involved in an X-rated film?

I made *Tropic of Cancer*, which was X-rated. It was a damn good film. Henry Miller and I were good friends. We used to play Ping-Pong together. He usually won. He said, "You don't have the guts to make *Cancer*." I got it made, and they pulled it after one theater, it was so rough. Ellen Burstyn was in it. She had a different name: Ellen McGray. She had her pussy showing, lice in her pussy, open legs. When Gulf & Western saw it, they said, "Get rid of this crazo." They made another picture they had to pull called *Medium Cool* with Haxell Wexler. It was so controversial that Gulf & Western wanted to get rid of that too. So when it came to *Last Tango*, they turned it down and I was sick about it. I was the one who got Marlon in it. It was a brilliant film. Maria Schneider came on at the last minute. Dominique Sander was supposed to play the part, but she got pregnant and Maria was Brigitte Bardot's stand-in. She was wonderful in that film, as good as Marlon. It was her first movie. I knew her well, used to take her out. She used to dance all alone at Costello's in Paris. What a body she had! Then she got stuck on heroin. When *Black Sunday* came around, she was up for that, she was a total dyke at that time.

After the success of Silence of the Lambs, *did you think back to* Black Sunday, *which was Thomas Harris's first novel?*

Sure. *Black Sunday* was the biggest disappointment of any picture I ever had. It cost me $6 million. I was offered that for my points. And I got a letter from the maven, Bernie Myerson, who said *Black Sunday* was going to be bigger than *Jaws*. It wasn't bigger than my jaw. But when it was shown to the exhibitors, they stood up and applauded like no other picture I've ever been involved with. Any film. I thought I had a winner. And I had thirty-seven points of it. Ended up not making enough money to make a phone call.

The reason: the Jews in America called me a Hitlerite in the *B'nai Brith Messenger*. I had to have guards around my house. The picture didn't play around the world. The Red Army of Japan threatened to blow up every theater in Japan if they played it in theaters around the world. The picture was pulled because it was so real. I showed both sides of the story. The Palestinian side and the Israeli side. And for the one scene where I show the Palestinian side, the sensitivities of the Jewish people were that strong they called me a Hitlerite.

Marathon Man and Black Sunday were made at the same time. Was there bad blood between Dustin Hoffman and John Schlesinger during Marathon Man?

Terrible. They never talked. There's a gag reel that I made that's locked up in a safe. I have it on a video. It was made for one reason: John Schlesinger did not want Dustin Hoffman in the film. He thought he was too old. The reason he really didn't want him was six years earlier Dustin had to screen-test for *Midnight Cowboy* and was paid $60,000, now he was making $2 million.

Dustin is a very difficult actor to work with. Two days before *Tootsie* opened Dustin called Sidney Pollack the bum director of the decade, in front of everybody.

Is it true that you sold Tootsie to your brother?

I gave *Tootsie* to him. It wasn't called *Tootsie*, it was called *Would I Lie to You?* My brother was looking to do something in his life. He was bored in New York. He had a terrible tragedy in his life. His wife and two children were burned to death in 1975. He was just a shambles of a person, which was understandable. He was hit with a baseball bat in the balls. He can never recover from it. And I wanted to give him some joy and do something that would turn him on. We used to go away to Palm Springs on weekends, and I wanted to get him involved in something, and I had this script that Dan McGowan had written. It was owned by a theater owner and had been around a long time. I read it after Buddy Hackett sent it to me. I said to Charlie, "This is a very funny piece of material." And he bought it, not from me, from Dan McGowan. At that time George Hamilton was going to do it. George went into the film business because of me. He became an actor because he said, "If Evans can be an actor, anybody can." He was a pool boy at the Beverly Hills Hotel. We're very good friends. I love George. He's underestimated as a performer. He's a very good comedian. Great personality.

Anyway, Dustin Hoffman was going to do the Renee Richards story. He wanted to do a transvestite story. And Dustin's a tennis player. Someone sent him *Would I Lie to You?* And Dustin liked it. My brother was the executive producer on it. I was happy for him.

Who are your five closest friends?

I don't want to say. But of the top ten, seven are women. Of the top three, it would be one woman and two men. Three women and two men are my five. And fifteen out of twenty are women, and I wish it wasn't that way. Because I do business with men.

During the making of *The Cotton Club* I had to get $2 million to pay the weekly payroll. Money was due to me from Orion the following Thursday, but money had to be paid that Friday. I went to four men to ask them for the loan, guaranteed by Orion the following Thursday, and all four—each of whom I had made $100 million for or more—gave me an excuse why they couldn't give it to me. The first two women I went to gave it to me before I finished the sentence and asked me if I wanted more. Liv Ullmann and Cheryl Tiegs. I rest my case.

What woman have you loved most?

How can I say? Ali, because we're locked at the hip, we've had a kid together. We shared magic together for two years with *Love Story*. She's in my life. She's in my will. Of my three best friends she's one of the three. And I am to her. In her book she said the one 911 number she has in her life is Robert Evans.

None of your four marriages worked out. [Evans married three more times after we talked. They also didn't work out, though he's still married — but living separately — to number seven.] How difficult are you to live with?

I'm a romantic. All of my marriages put together were less than seven years. I'm easy to live with, that's not the problem. Of my four wives, three of them are my best friends. My son Josh and I were having lunch at the Beverly Hills Hotel in the coffee shop downstairs, and Camilla, my wife before Ali, was sitting at the other end. Joshua had never met Camilla. She came up, and I introduced them, and Joshua said to her, "What kind of husband was my daddy? Because I never grew up having him as a father living with my mother." She said, "That's a very impertinent question, Joshua." He said, "I'd like to know from someone who was married to him, since my mother can't answer that question for me." She thought and she said, "Your father was the single worst husband any woman could *ever* be married to. However, he spoiled me for the rest of my life for any other man."

All my wives are lovely girls. I was very good to all of them. My priorities were just fucked in life. I don't like a structured life. I'm not a good social planner. I was a flagrant cheat—all the time. That's why my marriages couldn't work out, because I couldn't lie. Camilla found out that I was having many affairs. She didn't want to break up the marriage, but she asked me to at least see a psychiatrist. I didn't want to, but she asked as a favor to her, for dignity. So she sent me to one, and after the third visit he called Camilla and told her to forget it, to go out and have an affair because I was no good and would never change. For better or worse, I'm not a married type.

Do you still feel that the older you get the less you understand women?

No, I just think that they are more intuitive than we are, brighter than we are. Whether it be a country, an army, a team, a business, a family, a person—it's only as good as its weakest link. And every man has the same weak link: ego. Women don't have that. A good example: You're married to a girl, and she's out cheating every day. When you get in bed at night, you can't think she's fucking around because, "She's married to me, how can she do it?" Reverse: You're living with a woman and you fuck around. The first day you fuck she touches you and she can feel it, she knows it. A man doesn't because of his ego. A woman doesn't have that.

How many times I've gone to pick up some of the

most beautiful women to take them out, and they won't even go out because they think they look awful. They don't, they look beautiful. But I always think I look great! If a woman knows how to be fetching as a woman, that's the strongest asset in the world. There's a saying that has nothing to do with sex: The hair on a woman's pussy is stronger than the Atlantic cable. And it's true.

Look at Sherry Lansing. There's not one person who leaves her office who isn't charmed by her. And charmed by *noes*, not just *yeses*. Stanley Jaffe says Sherry is the best closer of any person he's ever known in the industry. Not that she's that brilliant. She knows how to use her femininity, and she's as tough underneath as anyone in the world.

Jack Nicholson has an expression: "Hey, Bob, don't try to figure them out. You can't, they don't play fair." That's a way to look at it.

How would you describe yourself?

I'm a loner. I enjoy being alone. I'd rather be remembered than be rich. And I'm an easy mark: I give to too many people.

After spending the morning with Evans at his office on the Paramount lot, he asked me to come to his house that evening at 11:30 PM to continue our talk. Evans is an insomniac who works while most of us sleep, but I thought that, with a few hours to rest, I could deal with it. However, at 10:00 PM he called to say he was still in the editing room at Skywalker Studios and would be there most of the night. Could I come at ten the next morning?

His house is above Sunset, behind the Beverly Hills Hotel. When I arrived, his butler took me through the main house and into the projection room, which is sandwiched between his oval swimming pool and the tennis court. The pool, the projection room, and the court probably contain more Hollywood history than any other house in the Beverly Hills-Brentwood-Bel Air triangle. Evans was late, so I had an opportunity to admire the Picasso and Toulouse-Lautrec prints, the nude drawings by Jean Negulesco, the view of the tennis court. I tried out the leather chairs he had designed, the ones that replaced the chairs taken by Jack Nicholson. I looked at the framed pictures and articles about Evans. And when he arrived, he showed me another: a Polaroid of his caricature from the Palms restaurant, with the words "The Robert Evans" next to it.

"I'm the only one who has that," he said about "The." "It might work as a title to your piece. It's just a thought."

Evans is a man of boundless energy. He likes to hum when he isn't concentrating, and during the next seven hours he would go between his house and the projection room at least a dozen times, humming as he walked, humming as he approached. It's easy to sense his presence before he actually arrives.

When his assistant came in, he asked her to tell me what she thought of him. "I would describe him as the most generous person, man or woman, that I have ever met in my entire life," she said, speaking like a loyal employee. "He's like nobody I've ever known. I would stop a bullet for him, because he gives and he gives and he gives. And it doesn't really matter who it is. He gives unconditionally. And everybody is still his friend because he is such a wonderful guy, how could you not like him? But he drives me crazy because I worry about him. After the smoke clears, he's giving everything away and he's standing there with his finger in his mouth. And it bothers me that people don't recognize what a sweetheart he is, and just back off sometimes."

During our first talk we concentrated on his tenure as vice president in charge of production at Paramount between 1966 and 1974. There was much more ground to cover, including his stint as an "independent" producer—the period that culminated with his bust for cocaine use and the disastrous *Cotton Club* episode that almost destroyed him. His production designer Richard Sylbert said that he had never seen Evans as anxious as he was at that time. "It wasn't just a fear of failure but the big fear of going into the toilet for the last time. He was a man who would do anything. He was in very deep shit."

But in spite of the failure of *The Cotton Club*, Evans managed to come out of that very deep shit. He's a man loaded with ideas, always running on a full tank, hoping to catch the magic once again. And he's not afraid to say what he thinks in an industry that usually prefers to keep the lid on what goes on behind the scenes.

Oh, by far. More than just a great art form, it's something else. All of us should be proud of this: It is the only product that is manufactured in the U.S. that is No. 1 in every country in the world. The American film flies the American flag higher than any other thing made in this country, and yet we don't even get any respect for it. You can laugh at Hollywood, but that's bullshit. People should praise Hollywood for what it's done. It's done a lot more than Detroit or Pittsburgh or Houston and Dallas have done in cars, steel, oil. The Japanese can't make our product, that's why they have to buy our companies. No one can duplicate the American film. I'm very proud of that. Being in an industry that's No. 1 in America, I don't understand why we don't get more government help, why there aren't schools that are set up for kids to learn, like engineering and doctors.

They should be undergraduate schools. There are so many people who have been in this industry a long time who would love to be professors, teachers, who could teach the art of making film. And so many young people want to learn it. I'm a full professor at Brown University. I taught a class there on the anatomy of film four times a year, and I never graduated high school. But no one else could teach my course. And they resented having to make me a professor. But more kids took my course than any other in the entire curriculum. Young people are hungry to learn about film, and there's no one there to teach them. It is definitely an art form, and it is definitely something that no one can knock us off on, because no one can duplicate the American film.

Growing up, did you have any heroes?

Dr. Jonas Salk is my greatest hero. Because he discovered the cure for polio. When I grew up, polio was rampant. I had kids all around me die or become paralyzed. One summer my mother thought I had it because I had a high temperature, I was throwing up. They closed all the pools, and all the kids couldn't play. Years later, when Salk moved to Palo Alto to work on the immunization of the cell, I wanted to quit Paramount and work for him. I went up to visit him several times, but there was nothing I could contribute except be in awe. He is my hero in life. I was sure he was going to come up with the cure for cancer. He was like my god, Salk.

When you were younger, did you have ambitions to get into the movies?

I was a kid actor for many, many years. I was under contract to Paramount. When I was eleven years old, I was an actor for radio. I was assigned to a picture when I was 17, called *City Across the River*, at Universal, but I got sick, my lung collapsed, and I couldn't do the part.

When your lung collapsed, did you think you might die?

Well, I was leading a wild life as a kid. My parents always backed me, what I wanted to do. Against their friends' advice. My father was a dentist, and all his friends were doctors and lawyers. In those days, when a kid wanted to be an actor, he was looked at as very peculiar. But I was a loner, I didn't play with the other kids. The only reason I wanted to be an actor was so I wouldn't have to face other kids. I always had a good voice, and I did accents very well. I became "the Accent Kid." I played Nazis during World War II on radio. Dicky Van Patten and I used to work together a lot. Dicky's father was a bookie. We used to go up to the Red Rooster in Harlem. There was a whorehouse upstairs and gambling downstairs. We went up with Alfred Lunt's valet. We went for the fascination, because all the girls would pick up their tips with their pussies. And in the eyes of a 15-year-old kid, this was something!

I fought on a bet with Dicky. One guy offered me on a dare to fight in the Golden Gloves. I said I was an actor, he bet me $100. So I went into the ring, and after two rounds I couldn't lift my arms. The next thing I knew I was out cold for thirty minutes, they thought I was dead.

But I was very busy as a kid actor. One time I was making more money than my father. And things were tough in those days, too.

At 14 weren't you earning $1,500 a week as a radio actor?

Some weeks. Some weeks less. Then everything dropped out from under me. After my lung collapsed, I couldn't get a job. I became a disc jockey in Palm Beach, then in Miami, then I was invited to Havana, Cuba. By disc jockey...it was a show in the lounge of the Copacabana Hotel. I gambled there and probably would have stayed a professional gambler if it wasn't for not wanting to disappoint my family. I didn't want them to be hurt by my behavioral patterns.

But this business is made up of gamblers: the Louis

B. Mayers, the Schencks, Harry Cohn. Darryl Zanuck was busted because of gambling, he had to borrow money from Howard Hughes. David Selznick used to play gin for a buck a point. So did I. I played with Richard Brooks, Willie Wyler, Sam Spiegel. In poker I played with Brooks, Doc Simon, heavy big games. You have to be a gambler to be in this business. To be in a position to put up $20 million on the seat of your pants, because there's no close out value. It's like Vegas, you drop it. Unlike a car, which you can close out if it doesn't sell, a film is like a parachute jumper: If it doesn't open, you're dead. You've got to be a gambler.

Your grandfather was a gambler, wasn't he?

He was a degenerate gambler. He'd go out for breakfast and come back three weeks later. He used to win and lose families. It was when there was no money in the family that my father became a dedicated professional. My father wanted to be everything his father was not. I wanted to be everything my father was not, even though I loved him very much. He was so dedicated to a structured family that I wanted to enjoy the celebration of life.

Havana during that time must have been a wild city.

It was the wildest place in the entire world. It was like *Godfather II.* I had to make a very quick exit from Cuba, because I was witness to something I shouldn't have been, which I cannot get into to this day. I don't want to talk about it. I was interviewing Abbe Lane on the radio, and I was brought into a room, blindfolded, taken out and put on a seaplane, landed in Miami on a desolate beach, given $10,000, and told never to come back again.

Was this the government kicking you out or a private party?

I'm not saying who did it. I was 17. I had a gun to my head. I shit in my pants, but I didn't talk. That's the truth.

So what did you do when you returned to New York? Is that when you joined your brother Charles in the clothing business?

No, my brother was out of a job at that time. When I came back to New York, I tried to get work in radio, couldn't get much work. I took a job as a male model in a clothing firm. I wanted to get in film. I wound up out in California handling a clothing line and got signed by Paramount Pictures. It was called the Golden Circle then, they had forty actors under contract. They signed me for $125 a week, and they taught me fencing and riding. I was under contract for six months, and they dumped me.

My brother by then started a little company called Evan Picone, and we decided to go into the pant business instead of making skirts. That was my job: to start women wearing pants in America. I'm very proud of it. Racks of pants weren't allowed in stores in those days, so I had to convince buyers that women would wear pants. I went all over the country doing this. Our whole factory was the size of my office here. I started a fashion that's a lot more important that most movies I've ever made, and it's something that will remain long after I'm dead. In the fifties women weren't allowed to wear pants. Jackie Kennedy in the sixties wasn't allowed in certain restaurants because she had pants on. It was taboo, considered insulting to fashion. I got women to wear pants, and I'm as proud of that as anything I've ever done.

Do you feel you have anything in common with Adolph Zukor or Sam Goldwyn, both of whom started in the clothing business?

No. They started as poor immigrants. I was an established person. I was an actor for a decade before I was in the clothing business.

You were "discovered" twice: first by Norma Shearer, who wanted you to play her husband, Irving Thalberg, then by Darryl Zanuck. Most hopefuls wait a lifetime to be discovered once. Were you just born under a lucky star?

If I weren't prepared for my discoveries, I wouldn't have gotten it. If I hadn't paid my dues. Being discovered is bullshit, you've got to be prepared for it. Luck is when opportunity meets preparation. I tested for both parts, they weren't given to me. Certainly I was lucky to have been discovered. But if I couldn't back it up, it would have been hello and goodbye.

How nervous were you acting with James Cagney in your first feature, Man of a Thousand Faces?

[Gets up again to look for an old Reader's Digest *article that quotes Cagney but can't find it.*] Cagney was my favorite actor. In my autobiography, the second chapter deals with going to see *Angels with Dirty Faces* as a kid and then going out and hitting a guy because I was trying to act like Jimmy Cagney. And here was my first experience as a professional actor, having to tell Jimmy Cagney how to act. They picked the wrong scene to start with! What happened was, I walked on to the set, and my father had come out, he was so proud, especially after all the shit he had taken from his friends, and I couldn't open my mouth. They did six takes. Cagney tells the story in *Reader's Digest*, he walked over to me and said, "Let me tell you something, kid. I'm 5 foot 4. The first scene I had was with a guy who was 6 foot 3. When the scene was over, I was 6 foot 3 and *he* was 5 foot 4. Don't be scared, just do it."

Why didn't Ernest Hemingway like you for The Sun Also Rises?

I didn't blame him. Why should he want me in the picture? He wanted a real bullfighter. I was a laugh. He and Peter Viertel both said: "Pedro Romero? You? No way, not in my story you're not." No one wanted me in the picture, and yet I got all the reviews. [*Takes down a framed Time review that says a "handsome" Evans displayed a "fierce intensity."*]

Did you get to meet Hemingway?

I saw him at the World Series after the picture opened. I walked over to him, and he said, "Good work, kid," and turned his head.

Was Hemingway an imposing figure?

Very.

Why did Darryl Zanuck come to your defense?

It's called a sense of discovery. There's an ego involved with it. Not that I was the best person for it, but he found me. I was *his.*

When I was on *The Sun Also Rises*, a telegram went out to Darryl Zanuck, who was in London; we were in Mexico.

The telegram read: IF ROBERT EVANS PLAYS PEDRO ROMERO THE SUN ALSO RISES WILL BE A DISASTER. SIGNED: ERNEST HEMINGWAY, HENRY KING, AVA GARDNER, TYRONE POWER, MEL FERRER, EDDIE ALBERT, PETER VIERTEL. Errol Flynn refused to sign it. Word comes back that Darryl Zanuck is flying in, and I'm told to report to the *corrida* to do my *quitas* and *veronicas*. I'm sure I'm going to get fired. So I walk into the arena, there's Zanuck on one side, on the other is Ava Gardner, Tyrone Power, and everyone else, and Zanuck is a little guy with a cigar sticking out of his mouth—he had only met me once, when I was dancing at the El Morocco. I go through my motions with a fake bull, bow to him, and Zanuck takes a megaphone and says: "The kid stays in the picture. And anybody who doesn't like it can quit." Puts the megaphone down and walks out. And that's what a producer is: a boss.

And my whole life has been fighting to stay in the picture, one way or another.

Was that an epiphany for you? You saw all the actors, and you saw the power of the producer...

Exactly! I wanted to be him and not me. That's when I made up my mind. My life goes back to the old studio days as an actor. I was under contract for Universal for a while, for Paramount, for Fox. I've been a radio actor, a stage actor, a film actor. I've done everything in this industry. And I love to work with actors. They're very bright. I learn from actors. They're contributors. I'm the only actor who has ever run a studio. And I lasted longer than anyone else in that job, I had total control.

Before we get back into that, did you date and fuck both Ava Gardner and Lana Turner?

I don't want to talk about that. But I was with both of them, yes. I can show it to you right here. [*Takes another framed set of clippings down from the wall, this one from a 1957 Journal-American, written by Dorothy Kilgallen, with the headline: "Bob Says Yes to Lana," and from another publication showing him with Ava Gardner sharing a table at a night club.*]

Was this when Photoplay voted you New Star of 1957?

Yes. Next to Elvis Presley, I was getting more fan mail than anyone at 20th Century Fox. For about five minutes I was very hot.

Did you know Elvis?

Oh sure. We went to a Halloween party together, we played softball together. We were both under contract to Fox. He was a very sweet guy. We didn't hang out a lot, but we knew each other. I liked him a lot.

Were women falling all over him?

He was very modest about it. He wasn't aggressive in any way. A country sort of kid.

You appeared in only two other films: The Best of Everything and The Fiend Who Walked the West. Anything memorable about either of them?

Very memorable. The best thing I ever did was a remake of *Kiss of Death*, which made Richard Widmark a star. It was called *The Hell-Bent Kid*, which they changed to *The Fiend Who Walked the West* three weeks before the picture opened. I was going to be the new big star at Fox as the Hell-Bent Kid. Edward R. Murrow interviewed me on his show because of it, and he only interviewed the biggest stars. They changed the title because they felt that westerns and horror pictures were big. I said, "You can't do this to me." I went to see Charlie Einfeld, the second-highest-paid guy at Fox, head of advertising and PR and distribution. I said, "You can't change the title, I wouldn't have made the film. He said, "You act in them, kid, let me sell 'em." I said, "But you're ruining my career." He said, "Two nights before the picture opens I want you to walk into El Morocco and smack a broad across the face. And I'll say, 'The fiend that walked the West is in New York.'" I said, "Are you crazy? I'm not going to smack a girl." He said, "Bogie used to do it for me in the forties." I said, "Fuck Bogie! I ain't doing nothing." He said, "You're going to have to make a trailer for it." I said, "Put someone else in the trailer, I'm not going to make it." And I walked out of his office. When the picture opened I got terrific reviews, but who looks at the reviews of a picture called *The Fiend Who Walked the West*? When it's on TV now, Warren Beatty always calls me and imitates me.

Why, after only four films, did you decide to quit acting?

Because I had to make a choice. Our business, Evan Picone, had grown very big. It was over a five-year period, and I was spending nine months of the year in California. I was signed to do two pictures, *The Chapman Report* and

The Longest Day. I turned down *Murder, Inc.*, the third lead, because I wanted the lead, which was given to Stewart Whitman. Actor's ego. I said, why should he have the lead? I'm a bigger actor than he is. The guy they hired to take my part was later nominated for an Academy Award for it: Peter Falk. It was his first movie. I also turned down *The Rise and Fall of Legs Diamond*, *The George Raft Story*, a lot of pictures. The parts I wanted I didn't get, the parts I was offered I didn't want. And my brother and his partner, Joe Picone, came to me and said, "Look, you're spending nine months of the year in California, and you're not in the business at all, it's not fair to us. Either sell out your interest in the business or come back and work for the company." They were right. I looked at myself in the mirror—and this was as tough a decision as I've ever had to make, and sometimes it's really tough to look at yourself and call a spade a spade—I said to myself, "You ain't good enough to make it all the way. You ain't gonna be Paul Newman. You're not that good an actor." So I gave up my contract, turned down the two pictures I was supposed to do, and moved back to New York selling ladies' pants. It was the single best decision I ever made in my life.

Even though you were getting so much fan mail?

I was much hotter with fan clubs than I was with producers and directors. One of the reasons was, I was a known commodity before I came to California. If I would have come as a garage man or a plumber or a carpenter...but when you're successful in another field and you become an actor, they hold it against you. You're really a hybrid. But I would be working as a waiter at Hamburger Hamlet now if I stayed as an actor.

You mean you have a better shot at becoming a legend as a producer than you would have as an actor?

A legend is someone who dies before his time. Why is it that Irving Thalberg is remembered and Louis B. Mayer isn't? Why is it that Marilyn Monroe is remembered where other actresses with a lot more talent aren't? Why is it that James Dean, who made only three pictures, is the largest-selling poster in the world? Because he died before his time. You outlive your legend many times and fade into either wealth or obscurity. But there's a certain time when you hit heights, and if you disappear at that time, you're remembered.

Why is an actress more than a woman and an actor less than a man?

The man who told me that was Henry Kissinger. The easiest girl to get to, to fuck, is the wife or girlfriend of a movie star or an actor, whether he's the biggest movie star in the world or an extra. Because invariably the woman he's with becomes his mother. He's that involved with himself, and he can't help it. It's no one's fault. But as an actor you need protection, and the woman you're with becomes your old lady. And after a while, when she's depended upon to do everything, including tying his shoelaces, the woman gets bored with it.

Conversely, a woman needs that same protection as an actress. Really, they're both the same. But in a woman it's attractive, it gives a man a macho feeling to give her that umbrella for protection. Actresses are so unsure of themselves, so insecure, that they come to the man for protection, and it makes him feel good. So on a man, as an actor, it's unattractive, but on a woman it makes her man feel good. Acting is basically a female trait, from makeup to fantasizing, it's not a male trait. That doesn't mean that actors aren't masculine. They are, but it's still narcissism and self-aggrandizement. Very few actors use dope because they're too concerned with their bodies. A lot of actors are alcoholics, though. That's the main thing with actors: They're afraid to face the world, so they become alcoholics.

Why do actors need more protection than people in other professions?

An actor feels, when he finishes a project, it's always his last job. I don't care who it is, unless you're a huge star. Feels like he'll never work again. And it eats him up inside. Invariably they're only happy when they're working. Where you don't have to face the world. It's like going on location is summer camp. It's a different world. And you get more and more into that until you can't face the world.

In the old days, actors were under contract to studios who dressed them, made them up, had cars to take them around. Once they were dropped, they didn't know how to face the world, they either committed suicide or became alcoholics. Stars like Robert Taylor: When he was dropped by MGM, he couldn't face the world, as big a star as he was. They didn't know how to function outside the studio system.

Conversely, today there's no such thing as a studio system. But as an actor, the more you become addicted to it, the more you live your own life, and you're always fearing you're never going to work.

As Zanuck had with you, have you also had that sense of discovery with others?

Oh sure I have. It's a big ego trip. I've had it many times. I go to bat for people all the time. And I stick by my convictions. Sometimes I'm right, sometimes I'm wrong. But you have to be wrong in order to be right. You can't bat a thousand. If you do, you're doing something wrong. You've got to take chances.

You took a chance with Popeye, which didn't meet the expectations many had for it. Didn't you want Dustin Hoffman, with Hal Ashby directing, until you and Hoffman had a falling out?

I had Dustin, and we had a big falling out because he wanted to fire Jules Feiffer as the writer and I refused. He said, "You're going with Jules Feiffer over me?" And I said, "That's right, because you're not giving him a fair shot." He had an epileptic fit with me, he was furious. Hal was willing to let Feiffer go, I was not. I believe in the writer. The man devoted nine months of his time, and Dustin did not give him enough time, kept him waiting for two and a half days. I lost the picture with Dustin.

You and Dustin didn't speak for six months?

Longer. And our friendship has never been the same. I feel badly about it because he's a very interesting character. We used to play tennis together. He gave me my tennis chair, because of all the bad calls. He still never won after the chair was there. He's a good player, too, but he's not a winner. Jack, Dustin, and I have approximately the same game. Jack and I are gutter players. I beat Dustin forty-eight out of fifty times, and Jack beats me forty-eight out of fifty times, and Dustin looks like he could beat us both forty-eight out of fifty times.

Do you think Popeye would have been any different had Hoffman and Ashby done it instead of Robin Williams and Robert Altman?

The real problem was, it shouldn't have been a musical. The reason it was a musical was because I had tried to buy *Annie.* They paid $10 million for *Annie.* Popeye was the third most recognizable face in the world. I loved the idea because it said something very strongly: I am what I am. The celebration of the individual. Robin was wonderful in it. It was his first movie. It's a much better picture than people give it credit for. People watch it and tell us they love it now. Shelly Duvall was great in it.

Was the problem also a lack of special effects? Did the money run out?

That was nothing. By the way, it wasn't a failure, it was a successful film. But not a *huge* success. If it were made not as a musical, it could have been very successful. But because of *Annie...*

During our talks, Evans received calls from Colleen Camp, who is married to John Goldwyn, from Stanley Jaffe, and from his brother Charles. Apparently Goldwyn was blaming Charles for holding up a deal because Goldwyn believed that Evans couldn't make a deal without his brother's permission. Evans admitted that he had had to borrow money from his brother—"So he has a security interest in what I have, nothing wrong with that. I don't want anything for nothing. But it gets back to Paramount that I can't make a deal without his permission. That's how the politics are at the studios. You heard me talk to Stanley Jaffe, the chairman of the board. I just won't take any shit from anyone. Because I have nothing to hide. I learned early in life, when you lead as complicated a life as I do, nothing to do with morality, the easiest thing is to tell the truth. Then you never have to remember what you said. I can walk into any room, whether there are ten people or three hundred, and I don't have to remember what I said to any one of them. I say it as it is. People may like it or not like it, but they can't say I'm a liar. It just makes life easier."

How dark a business is the movie business? Outsiders see the glamour. You're on the inside. What do you see?

There's no glamour in this business. There're accountants, lawyers, agents. For every bit of magic, you spend a month of misery in negotiations. It's not glamorous. By the time you start a film, you're tired out. And things get made for the wrong reasons. And you fight on everything. There's more money taken out of the pie for legal in this industry than there is in any other industry. It's not the agents who hurt the business, it's the lawyers. The agents want to close deals, they pay their light bills that way. The lawyers find reasons to build up bills, so they always find things that are wrong. At my table at home Bob Towne, Jack Nicholson, and I put out our hands, we were going to make *The Two Jakes* for nothing. I was going to costar and produce with Jack, and Bob was going to direct and write it. And no agents and no lawyers were going to fuck it up. We put blood to it. And it got fucked up over lawyers and agents. Even working for nothing. We were all going to take no money up front.

If that would have happened, we would have started a new trend in films, where the above-the-line people would take no money. That's the way films should be made, because then you could make double the amount of films. Because when your above-the-line is so heavy, all the rest goes up too. We were going to make *The Two Jakes* for $11 million, with Jack, myself, Bob Towne, Harvey Keitel, Kelly McGillis, and Cathy Moriarty.

Why should somebody get paid $15 million for a film and the picture dies? That's why, on the other side, the studios cheat you. They have to. You can't give away 50 percent of the profits and incur 100 percent of the losses.

That's why you have fancy bookkeeping. When you're overly paid, as we all are, you can't have it both ways. You can't be independent and be overly paid.

When it appeared you weren't going to be acting in it, was Dustin Hoffman ever considered to take your role opposite Nicholson?

No. We couldn't accommodate both of them. The other part wasn't that big, it was like eight scenes. I didn't want to do it. Bob Towne insisted. It was his father, it's a true story. It was boomtown right after World War II, where all the Jewish entrepreneur real-estate guys, the Mark Tapers, came in to build, like his father did. Where the Gentiles had all the oil, the Jews were doing business in real estate. And Jack said in front of Bob Towne, Bert Fields, Ned Tanen, Frank Mancuso: "Listen clearly, gentlemen. I will make *The Two Jakes* for nothing, with Evans. Otherwise, I want $6 million without him. And Towne, I'll buy your screenplay for $2 million and you get out. Because you know what's going to make this picture? The Irishman isn't dumb. Our noses [Evans's and Nicholson's] next to each other, that's what's going to make this picture." That's loyalty. Let me show you the pictures we took. [*Shows me large photos taken by Helmut Newton of Nicholson and himself in profile, their noses close to touching.*]

What did you think of the end results of The Two Jakes?

Sad. Bob Towne never turned in a screenplay. He terribly resented Jack directing it. But it was the only way we could do it. He didn't want to direct it. We had a $4 million encumbrance against us because we had our own money up for it. There were lawsuits and everything, and he wanted to clean the slate. He worked his ass off on it, and I was of no help to him, I was a vegetable at the time. He was so kind. I didn't show up on the set because I was embarrassed and ashamed because of the stuff going on in the papers. To keep me involved in the picture he would bring the cinematographer and other crew members to come here and watch dailies rather than see them in the studio. He did that throughout the entire picture.

Would Nicholson ever want to direct again?

I don't know. He's such a big movie star. He said to me he so much wanted me in the part. Mike Nichols, who was going to direct it, wanted me. It was such a bad time for me because this was right after *The Cotton Club*. The drug thing happened in 1980. *The Cotton Club* was '80 to '84, then *The Two Jakes*, then this Roy Radin case blew up in my face, which had absolutely nothing to do with me. But it did, I made publicity, I made it a celebrated thing, without me it was nothing. I had ten years of Kafka.

Let's talk about those years. Your brother and a friend were caught in New York buying cocaine from an undercover cop. You were in California at the time, yet you admitted to buying into the score. Were you guilty?

I was totally innocent of the charges. I took a dive. But I don't want to get into it. I was guilty of usage, but innocent of the charge. It was the most costly non-blow in the history of the world. If I had to do it again, I wouldn't do it. I never realized the consequences. Robert Redford, Warren Beatty, or Tom Cruise wouldn't have gotten bigger headlines. And the headlines I got around the world, it was above the name of the paper. And I had nothing to do with it! [Shows me a scrapbook devoted to articles on his drug bust.] Aljean Harmetz in the New York Times wrote what happened, and said I wasn't there. This made me the Cocaine Kid when I wasn't involved.

Did you save your brother and his friend?

Oh yes, I did. But I never thought it would have the devastating effect it did. To this day, let's say I'm at the Palm restaurant and I have to take a piss. I'll piss in my pants before I'll go to the john. Because if I go people will think I'm taking a snort. And I have pissed in my pants rather than go to the john. That will stay with me for the rest of my life. However, during it, I did something that shows that sometimes good comes from bad. I did a show for NBC that turned NBC all around. It was *Get High on Yourself*. It started as a thirty-second commercial, which is what the judge asked me to do. And it became the biggest anti-drug campaign in the history of America. I had every big star in the world go on it.

But how does one stop the drug problem today?

The only way you can stop it is what we did. We did more in six months...let me get the tape and show it to you. Three weeks before it was going to go on the air I never thought people would show up for it, and everybody showed up: Paul Newman, Dr. J, Magic Johnson, Henry Winkler, even Bob Hope, who showed up for a guy who was copping a plea. From a thirty-second commercial it became a year and a half of my life. But it changed programming on television.

The drug agencies tried to disavow what we were

doing because we did more in six months than they did in twenty-five years. They couldn't do anything to me, so they went after Kathy Lee Crosby, who worked on it with me. They brought out she was a Scientologist and ruined her name, because they didn't want us to succeed in what we were going to accomplish. And I wasn't doing this for charity but to pay penance.

Now, I didn't intend to do what I did. All I had to do was have Henry Winkler go on and say, "Don't take drugs." That's all I had to do. But I don't do things that way, like an idiot. If the proudest thing I've done is about the Pope, this is the second thing.

Still, the question remains, how do you keep kids off drugs?

I'll tell you how. My son has never smoked a joint, never used drugs, doesn't drink. For one reason: He's goal-oriented. Kids have to have a goal. You can never stop drugs from coming in, it's greed, up to the highest levels of government. But you've got to give the kids an alternative.

Ten years ago it was very fashionable for the kids of the wealthy to take drugs. It's not that way anymore. Now it's the poorer neighborhoods, where they're needing it for survival, where big business is involved pushing it on kids to sell. Usage has gone down a lot in areas. Cocaine is not the fashionable drug to use anymore, which it was then. Now it's crack, and it's being sold by people right out of Washington, on the highest levels. That's why they don't stop it. It's called greed.

How high a level do you suspect it went? All the way to the top, to Ronald Reagan?

No, under that. Nancy Reagan picked up on our campaign and did her thing. But it was on high levels and various subcommittees and big lobbyists. Too much money is made from the importing of drugs into this country not to involve very important people who don't want to change. And it will never change by trying to stop it from coming in. They'll always figure out a way of getting it in.

What was your opinion of Reagan as president?

He was a brilliant communicator and a dreamer. He did, through strength, bring a cessation to the Cold War. I think he's very underestimated.

After that antidrug campaign you wound up in the headlines again when Roy Radin was killed. It was a sensational case that became known as "The Cotton Club Murder" because Radin was involved with you trying to raise money for your movie. And you were supposedly involved with the woman, Lanie Jacobs Greenberger, a drug dealer who is in prison today for her involvement in his death. Why did you refuse to testify at the preliminary hearing?

No one thought I was guilty of it. The police knew I wasn't guilty. They were pressing me to talk, and I had nothing to say. I would be in court, and there would be 150 photographers there. When I wasn't there, there weren't two photographers. I made careers for people when they had nothing on me. And I would not be intimidated.

Who was guilty in Radin's murder?

I don't know. I knew the person [Lanie Jacobs Greenberger],

but I don't know if she's guilty or not. But as horrible a person as she's supposed to be, she could have said something about me to cop a plea and she never did. She had nothing to say, but people can lie. And I had nothing to do with it, and thank God someone was honest about it. When you're a public figure, you're guilty until proven innocent, and I lived with that for eight years. I never opened my mouth, under advice of counsel, and that was the right thing.

Greenberger said she told you that Radin had been killed a week after it happened. Did she tell you?

I found out he was killed. To the best of my memory, I don't remember her telling me, but I don't want to be quoted in this because I have nothing to say about it. A murder case—she's in incarceration now. I don't wish to open up anything. I'm out of it. I've never spoken, I don't wish to speak about it.

What it did seem to show was how one might go to extremes to raise money to make a film.

I didn't need the money, I already had the money. It was all financed. We were in pre-production.

Wasn't Radin involved in helping you finance it?

No, no, not at all. He was trying to form a company of some kind. You know what it was, a media title: "The Cotton Club Murder." It had zero to do with The Cotton Club. None of them put up any money, and the movie got made, didn't it? It goes to prove it had nothing to do with The

had put up the money for the film. It was budgeted at $24 million, and they could have had a completion bond. I said, please take it. And Francis talked them out of taking it. It cost $47 million, and Francis put in half the film. After that preview I sat down and wrote him a letter, and Edward Doumani drove the letter from San Jose to Napa Valley. After Francis read the letter, he said, "This cocksucker is right, but I'd rather see the picture do $300,000 than $300 million and see that prick get credit for it."

What my letter said was exactly what Pauline Kael's review said three months later. [*Shows me the fifteen-page letter he sent to Coppola, criticizing his cut of the film. "What you are about to read bears great[er] consequence to our lives and careers than any decision we have ever fought over or agreed to in the past,"* he wrote. *Concerned that the previews had all gone badly, Evans wanted to change the movie, putting back scenes Coppola had cut, including seventeen musical numbers. "It is your film, Francis,"* he wrote, *"not mine. ...[But] not having communication [with you] at this very pivotal moment is so very counterproductive. My God, Francis, if Gromyko and Reagan can meet and have an exchange of dialogue, why can't we? You owe it to yourself if no one else to put personal feelings aside. Use me. Use my objectivity. ..."* The suggestions are numerous and detailed.]

Did you dictate this letter?

I wrote it in a hotel room in San Jose with the Doumanis standing by reading it. It was a painful letter to write. They agreed with me totally.

And were any of your suggestions taken?

None.

Did you speak to Coppola about this as well?

I never spoke with him. The written word is a far more powerful expresser of your thoughts: You're never interrupted, it stays with you, you can review it. I insisted that in my book they had to print this entire letter. People ask what is a producer: This letter gives you an answer.

Why didn't he listen to any of your suggestions?

I think he wanted the Doumanis to go bankrupt, and he'd take over the picture himself. Because what he did to those people is almost legally criminal. These poor guys were putting up money every day. He has ass-kissers around him that if he barks they think it's part of his genius. But the structure, he didn't have people. It's the same thing with *The Godfather*. No different.

What about The Godfather Part III? Which you had no hand in and it turned out to be a mess.

That's absolutely Francis, totally. End of story. That says it all. *Godfather III* was a tenth-generation Xerox copy of *The Godfather*.

Had he come to you for help on Godfather III, would you have worked with him?

Oh no, I would never talk to him again. Ever. Because he's an evil person. I think Al [Pacino] feels this way about him, too. Francis is a direct descendent of Prince Machiavelli. That's the best way I can say it. He's royalty. He is so seductive, so brilliant in his web of bringing people in, he makes Elmer Gantry look like Don Knotts. He fooled me. He's a brilliant director with actors, but he cannot structure a picture. Not just *The Cotton Club*. It took him three years to edit *Apocalypse Now*. It took him two years to edit *The Conversation*.

Did you ever have to write a letter like the one you wrote to Coppola to anyone else for any other film?

I had to go to this extent with *Sliver*, how about that? Even further. I will show you a letter that I wrote to Stanley Jaffe, chairman of the board at Paramount. He was so angry when he got this letter, the vein in his temple almost burst. Stanley was the one who gave me my break back. He opened the doors and embraced me. We're very close friends for twenty-five years. I'm the dishonorable godfather to his child. And I wouldn't meet with him until he read this letter, which I'll show you but you can't quote from it. Stanley faced me and he said, "Are you threatening me?" I said, "Yes, but I'm saving your ass, too." I had put my job on the line, I had to be willing to quit. He respected that without telling it to me. And whatever I wanted I got.

Can I mention that you wrote the letter?

You can say the passion I had brought me to write a letter on *Sliver*. That's okay. To the point of detriment I have a passion for what I do. I become possessed, more than obsessed. I strive to get something that can touch magic. And for the wrong reasons things happen: for distribution reasons, for lack of communication, for committees. I can't work that way. And unfortunately, I don't have enough money to put up my own money to make a picture and make it the way I want. As long as it's that way, I'm a dependent producer. But no one has the guts to do what I do. I'm not saying that's smart.

So the final cut of Sliver is your version, take it or leave it?

Seventy percent, not all. Enough. I went for the money shots. And Philip [Noyce] and I worked together as closely as two brothers.

How important is Sliver to you and your new career?

It's the most important picture of my career. Because I haven't really worked in ten years. I had very little to do with *The Two Jakes*. It was a gift to me. I wasn't in condition.

How do you compare it to Ira Levin's other work, Rosemary's Baby?

Roman Polanski is the most brilliant director I've worked with in my career. The subject matter isn't nearly as exploitable or as interesting as *Sliver*. *Rosemary's Baby's* subject matter was a cult, which isn't as interesting as voyeurism. But as a film, *Rosemary's Baby* is brilliant because of Roman. On *Sliver* I didn't have that brilliance, but it wasn't Phil's fault, he didn't have time. This picture was rushed. It was like making a sausage. We started in October and had to deliver it in April. It was crazy. Roman could never have done that, he wouldn't have accepted it. An artist needs time on the canvas.

What kind of look did you want for this one?

I wanted it to be like a European film from a woman's point of view. Sharon's character is the one that grows throughout the piece, and it's told through her eyes. I tried to put myself in her body.

Is Sliver equally as important to Sharon Stone as it is to you?

It's just as important to her. In this picture it's not Sharon Stone and Michael Douglas, it's Sharon Stone and two younger actors. She carries the picture. If it does what I think it's going to do, she'll be on a level all her own. She'll deserve as much as Tom Cruise. She'll raise the price of women in film. She'll get $10 million after this picture, and she deserves it. Thank God there are women who are getting parts now. It's much more difficult writing a woman's part than a man's part. A guy has props: guns, fights, planes, chases. A woman doesn't have that. She has mystery, and that's much more difficult to write than it is to write action. So a writer doesn't spend the time on women's roles. Faye Dunaway in *Chinatown* only had seven scenes, but you never forget them because they're so well written.

You once expressed a desire to go away with Robert Towne for a year and write the definitive erotic film. What would that be?

I think I've done an erotic film now: *Sliver.* And it's not a pornographic film.

Along the lines of Body Heat?

More. I'm not saying it's better, I love *Body Heat.* That was an erotic film.

How much do you stand to earn if Sliver does well?

I have a good piece of it. I don't have enough money to pay my state taxes now. How about that? I'm in debt. But I have a movie star deal. I deserve it. Of course, because you deserve it doesn't mean you get it [laughs].

With all your troubles the last ten years, how have you managed to survive?

I went broke. In 1979 I was a very wealthy man. The only money I earned during the entire decade of the eighties was as a male model for a cosmetics company from a picture that [Francesco] Scavullo took. I was paid several thousand dollars a month for that picture, selling women's cosmetics. I had to use the money that I saved. I sold my Gulf & Western stock. I made terrible financial decisions. But I didn't change my way of life.

Did you sell the rights to the films you had?

No, I get money from that, but it's nothing compared to my upkeep.

Did anyone offer to help you out?

Jack helped me out. Not monetarily, I'm too proud. My brother helped me, and I paid him back.

By 1989 you were contemplating suicide, and you put yourself into an insane asylum. Why?

I didn't think of committing suicide. I was afraid to.

My son could not get a date to his graduation because I was his father. That's how low I got. After this murder stuff came up, I became a media event, just like Roman [Polanski] did. I sold my home, and I was so depressed over it that I was just in a fetal position for months. I had a hundred Nembutal by my bed. If it wasn't for my son, I would have taken them. But rather than have that happen, I checked myself into the looney bin. But I escaped within twenty-four hours, I couldn't believe what I did. I'm not embarrassed to admit it, because if I can come back at my age, anybody can.

On my 62nd birthday, I was so depressed. Because that day, for some strange reason, *Man of a Thousand Faces* was on television, and I was 26 when that was made. My numbers were reversed. And I'm still waiting for the phone to ring. I was all alone, and Jack came around, and the two of us got loaded, just the two of us together until two in the morning. Loyalty's a very important word, and there's a very great shortage of it. You can give it, but don't expect it back. If you get it back one out of three times, you're doing well.

How close is your image to your real life?

People have various images of me. So many people have said they wanted to be me. I'm so many young guys' fantasy: To be Robert Evans one day. Robert Evans has not lived a happy life. I don't believe in happiness and unhappiness, I believe in being turned on and not turned on. Being turned on and doing something with passion is what my happiness is. That's not a normal happiness. I'm not a good parent. I never took my kid to Disneyland, because I wanted him to learn who I was. I read that in

Budd Schulberg's book about his father. His father just let him hang around. If I took my son to Disneyland, to the park, to the ball field, he knew I wouldn't be enjoying it. I let him hang around me, watching me cut films, and he learned to love me that way. I wasn't a good father, but we've been totally open, and now we're best friends.

Do you consider your book, The Kid Stays in the Picture, *a tell-all memoir?*

Not tell-all at all. I don't get into kiss-and-tell. But as an example, at Lew Wasserman's fortieth anniversary there were only forty people invited to his home. I was one of the forty. At his fiftieth anniversary, there were fifteen hundred people invited, I wasn't one of them.

And your book covers the years in between?

Oh sure, before, during, and after. Why my book has the opportunity of being more than an industry book is because when I started it, it didn't have a third act. Now it does. There's no such word as "impossible." In other words, the impossible dream is possible, but life itself has to be respected and protected, and if it's not, then that dream can turn into a nightmare. And to turn the nightmare back into a dream is impossible...almost. My story is: If I can come back at my age, I don't want to hear any kid at 25 or 30 saying he can't do it.

How much of a struggle was it for you to do the book?

It was painstaking. It was heavy therapy. I cried. The book is totally candid, totally. To the point that it hurt a lot. But if you're gonna do it, you want to do it all. It opens with the opening night of *The Godfather* and then goes backward to my life as a kid, and then it goes forward. I spent a year and a half on it.

When you turned 50, you said you didn't know who you were. You're in your 60s—do you know now?

When I turned 50, I didn't know where I stood. I went down for ten years at that time. I lived through *Rashômon*, and I got out of it at my age. And I'm proud of myself for doing that, not only for myself, but I can be an example to others. I didn't just get off the floor: I got off the floor as a cripple. And I never gave up.

Where are you going to be ten years from now?

I hope alive. And healthy. And I want to be busy. I have too good a mind not to use it. And I love what I do. I feel I'm a very wealthy man because of that. You know what I would really love, more than anything? The one thing that's evaded me, and I may never have it, but I sure would love it: peace of mind. I'd love to hear just crickets instead of phones. I'd love to have some silence in my life. I haven't had three weeks off in twenty years. And it's taken its toll.

Afterword
Saturday, January 25, 2008

"My stories are not only *not* exaggerated," Evans says to me fifteen years after our marathon conversation, "but they're underplayed. Because if I told the truth, no one would believe me." He is wearing a white robe over his clothes as we walk among the different rooms in his house. "That's how bizarre it is. I often wonder how I'm alive."

He has a right to wonder, because since we spoke he had a debilitating stroke that left his entire right side paralyzed—"from my eye to my tongue to my fingers," he tells me. "The doctor said, 'Get used to it, Evans.' The more he said, 'You'll have a different life,' the more I said to myself, 'Fuck you, you prick.'"

Discouraged by doctors, Evans found encouragement from his boss, and friend, Viacom CEO Sumner Redstone: "He'd gone through a terrible burn accident where he thought his life was over," Evans recalls. "A normal person would have died. He kept on saying to me as I was lying on the cot at Cedar's, 'If I made it, you can make it too! I don't want to hear you can't.'"

If it's beginning to sound like a scene out of a movie, where the crippled hero is pushed by a loved one into taking his first step, it gets even better for Evans. Not only did he recover from his stroke, but he made a life-changing decision—to get married—not once, but three times!

"I hadn't been married for twenty years when we spoke," he laughs. "Since my stroke I've been married three times. One was only for a few days, that doesn't count. Before my stroke I knew I'd never get married again. The stroke affected me. It does affect your brain."

Before the stroke, Evans' book, *The Kid Stays in the Picture*, had been a bestseller and a critical success, enough of one to make him want to write a sequel. He wrote most of it, but has gotten bogged down on the final chapters of *The Fat Lady Sang*, a title written with a nod to how the stroke hit him ("The Fat Lady sang and I thought I died. But luckily for me she forgot the last verse"). "I haven't finished the last part of the book," he says ruefully. "I don't know why. It's been two years since I put it aside."

Perhaps it's psychological, since the first book is a tough act to follow. "Writing it was terribly painful," Evans admits. "There wasn't a day I didn't cry at night."

In February 2004, *Publishers Weekly* included *The Kid Stays in the Picture* among their list of the six best books, not just of that year, but in general. The other five were *The Battle With Truth* by Albert Speer, *Democracy in America* by Alexis de Tocqueville, *The Prince* by Niccolò Machievelli, *A Midnight Clear* by William Wharton, and F. Scott Fitzgerald's *The Beautiful and the Damned*. They called Evans's book one of the best Hollywood memoirs ever written. The audio version became a must-listen-to in Hollywood, and a documentary was made from it.

"I had more gratification from the audio of my book than if I would have made *Titanic*," Evans says with pride. "It not only gave me pleasure, but quite frankly celebrity."

It had to have given him more pleasure than the movies he produced in the years since 1994. There was *Sliver*, which got terrible reviews but made money. "It did about $180 million around the world," he says. "It was important because I hadn't worked in a while, so it was my comeback. I didn't like the picture at all. I liked the beginning of it, but they fucked it up terribly."

There was *Jade*, with David Caruso and Linda Fiorentino in 1995, which lost money. "That picture should have been very good, but there were problems with the studio. When your balls are cut off it's tough to have a deep voice.

"We are in the media business today; I was in the film business. There's a difference. It was entertainment then. I was interested in every bit of minutiae of a film, from the collar an actor wore to his walk to his inflection to the continuity of his performance to the cut, the sound. I was too much of a perfectionist for a lost art. Today we're just puppets."

In 1996 came The Phantom and in '97 The Saint. Two characters with franchise potential that never made it to sequels. "The Saint was a much bigger picture than The Phantom. It did enough business to make it a franchise, but there was a lot of animosity between the leading man [Val Kilmer] and the studio." It was a huge disappointment for Evans, who put it out of mind when he had his stroke. The films he produced after he recovered were The Out-of-Towners with Steve Martin, Goldie Hawn, and John Cleese ("It wasn't bad, but I had very little to do with it") and How to Lose a Guy in 10 Days, with Kate Hudson and Matthew McConaughey.

"I had a lot to do with that. It made a lot of money. For what it was it was fine. Light fare. Nothing to brag about."

What he did like was what caused him the most grief: the animated Kid Notorious, which Comedy Central put up in 2003, with visions of an adult South Park. But it was cancelled after eight episodes, despite four-star reviews in the New York Post and three-page full-color ads in Rolling Stone and Vanity Fair. "That's the one that killed me. The best reviews of any picture I had since Chinatown. I loved the show, but I didn't want it to be as vulgar as South Park."

As disappointed as he was over the cancellation of Kid

Notorious, it pales in comparison to what happened to his fabled and beloved screening room, which was lost in a freak accident that left a gap in his heart.

"Brett Ratner, who lived with me while his house was being renovated, gave me a Sony plasma TV, and it exploded. It wasn't even on. It was seven o'clock in the morning. The screening room was all gone in thirty seconds! It didn't burn, it exploded. What I had in there was my history. I had original art, a Picasso. A thousand pictures...lost. It was the meeting place of everybody. It was the most painful loss, outside of human loss."

I follow him into his dining room. The table is filled with oversized photos by Helmut Newton. Some are of naked women, others are of Evans with Jack Nicholson, Evans with his son Joshua, and one is of a particularly attractive woman sitting in a seductive pose. "See this woman?" Evans says with a smile that brings back memories. "I had her. Years ago. Not bad, eh?"

Not bad at all. I look at the picture closely and throw out one of his favorite sayings, "Any man who can read the mind of a woman is a man who knows nothing."

Evans smiles again at me. "That's true," he says. "And I have a picture to prove it. It's the most important picture of my life. And that's saying a lot." He leads me to the hallway between the main entrance of his house and the kitchen, where hundreds of framed pictures take up every inch of space. There are photos of Evans at all stages of his life, from the handsome young bullfighter in *The Sun Also Rises* to the shots with him and Ava Gardner, Norma Shearer, James Cagney, Roman Polanski, Francis Ford Coppola, Sumner Redstone, Brett Ratner, Warren Beatty, Dustin Hoffman, Henry Kissinger, Alain Delon, Alfred

Hitchcock, Laurence Olivier, Barry Diller, Michael Eisner, Charlie Bluhdorn, Bob Hope, Sharon Stone, Faye Dunaway, Barbra Streisand, Clint Eastwood, and the Queen Mum. The picture that speaks ten thousand words though, the one he wants to show me to illustrate how a man can never penetrate the mind of a woman, is one of him and his then wife, Ali McGraw. It was taken at the St. Regis Hotel in 1972 after the first screening of *The Godfather*. It was, he says, the highest moment of his life. McGraw had flown in on a private jet to be with him. She has her arms around his neck, her hands extended, her face nestled in his. She is so proud of him. She is with her husband, the man of the hour, the producer of what would eventually become the American Film Institute's Greatest Film of All Time.

"Would you believe she was madly in love with another man, and I had no idea?" Evans says.

"Steve McQueen," I say, knowing the story from our previous conversation.

"That's right. She wanted to be with me like she wanted to be with a leper that night." Of course, you could never tell from that picture. Which is why Evans believes so strongly in the impossibility of ever understanding the opposite sex. "A man couldn't do that to a woman; but a woman can do that to a man," he says. And yet, when I ask him if there was a fire in his house and he could only grab one picture among the hundreds on the wall, he immediately points to this very shot.

"The one that broke your heart," I say.

"No, it didn't break my heart; it broke my spirit."

I don't ask for details. Some things are just too personal to press.

On the way back to the dining room we make a detour to his bedroom. "There are three sayings I have framed in my room. One is, 'The flare of the unexpected is what memorable is all about.' When you look back at your life, the things you remember are those things that were unexpected. The second is, 'Seduction: Creating an appetite and offering the potential for the fulfillment.' That's the truest statement ever made. If I had a sales organization of a thousand people I'd have this on their desks to read and memorize, because that's what it's all about: to create an appetite. Seduction comes into play every moment that you're awake. The third is, 'Try a thing three times. Once to get over the fear of doing it. Twice to learn how to do it. The third, to see if you like it or not.' That's Virgil Thomson who said it at the age of 93."

He then shows me two of his proudest possessions. One is a golden key to New York City now framed on the wall by the side of his bed. It was given to him by then Mayor Abe Beam in 1975, the year when *The Godfather Part II* came out. "I'm the only person in the movie business ever to get this," he says. And in the adjoining room he shows me what he's most proud of. It's not any award he received. It's not even about the movies. It's the framed 1976 certificate from Brown University granting him a full professorship. "I didn't go to college, I didn't get a B.A., I didn't get an M.A., I didn't get a PH.D. I didn't even finish high school. You can't become an Ivy League professor without a PH.D., but I got one. They gave it to me. If only my parents could have been around for that, because I was like the bad seed of the family. No one ever would have thought that I'd be sitting among the professors of Brown talking education. My life's a fairy tale. And this means more to me than if I got the Thalberg Award at the Oscars."

Never one to miss an opportunity, Evans had five

hundred 8-by-10 photos made of him as a Brown professor and used them when he met young women. "I'd give them the photo and say 'Don't tell your mother and father that you're going out with some dirty old producer.'" Spoken like a true academic!

He opens a closet door where many of the scripts, books, scrapbooks, and magazines featuring him are stored and picks up an old copy about Universal films, opening to a picture of him with James Cagney. Then he notices the binding of a *Great Gatsby* script. "Warren Beatty wanted me to play Gatsby," he says. "I told him he should do it and I'd direct." He stands in his white robe looking back on a lifetime of projects, some executed, most not. It's a closet filled with dreams and memories. "I'm looking for these pictures of this girl, this porno star, they were in here. I think someone must have stole them."

Evans leads me back to the dining room where he wants to sit, his back to the outside circular pool, which looks more like a small pond. Surrounding it are high rising jets of water that arc into the center of the pool. I stare at that fountain and smile to myself because it is raining outside, one of those rare L.A. storms. And yet the fountain remains on. I don't ask Evans about it...because some things are just too personal.

PUBLISHED BY RAT PRESS
RP001
FIRST EDITION OF 3000 PRINTED IN 2009
ISBN 978-0-9818056-1-0

PORTIONS OF THIS BOOK WERE PREVIOUSLY
PUBLISHED IN MOVIELINE,
AUGUST AND SEPTEMBER 1993.

PRINTED IN CANADA

WWW.LAWRENCEGROBEL.COM

DESIGN: FREE ASSOCIATION
WWW.FREE-ASSOCIATION.ORG

WWW.RATPRESS.COM